The Wisdom Trail

In the Footsteps of Remarkable Women

JANET LIEBERMAN

and

JULIE HUNGAR

THE PENGUIN PRESS

New York

2009

THE PENGUIN PRESS
Published by the Penguin Group
Penguin Group (USA) Inc., 375 Hudson Street,
New York, New York 10014, U.S.A. • Penguin Group (Canada),
90 Eglinton Avenue East, Suite 700 Toronto, Ontario, Canada M4P 2Y3
(a division of Pearson Penguin Canada Inc.) • Penguin Books Ltd,
80 Strand, London WC2R 0RL, England • Penguin Ireland,
25 St. Stephen's Green, Dublin 2, Ireland (a division of Penguin Books Ltd) •
Penguin Books Australia Ltd, 250 Camberwell Road, Camberwell,
Victoria 3124, Australia (a division of Pearson Australia Group Pty Ltd) •
Penguin Books India Pvt Ltd, 11 Community Centre, Panchsheel Park,
New Delhi—110 017, India • Penguin Group (NX), 67 Apollo Drive,
Rosedale, North Shore 0632, New Zealand (a division of Pearson
New Zealand Ltd) • Penguin Books (South Africa) (Pty) Ltd,
24 Sturdee Avenue, Rosebank, Johannesburg 2196, South Africa

Penguin Books Ltd, Registered Officers:
80 Strand, London WC2R 0RL, England

First published in 2009 by The Penguin Press,
a member of Penguin Group (USA) Inc.

LIBRARY OF CONGRESS CATALOGING-IN-PUBLICATION DATA

Lieberman, Janet.
The wisdom trail : in the footsteps of remarkable women /
by Janet Lieberman and Julie Hungar.
p. cm.
ISBN 978-1-59420-222-3
1. Women—United States—History—20th century. 2. Women—United
States—Social conditions—20th century. I. Hungar, Julie Yearsley. II. Title.
HQ1420.L49 2009
305.40973'0904—dc22
2009003553

Printed in the United States of America
1 3 5 7 9 10 8 6 4 2

DESIGNED BY AMANDA DEWEY

CONTENTS

Women of the Wisdom Trail

LORRAINE BEITLER	*Educator, historian, founder and curator of the Dreyfus project*
NELL BERRY	*Community and neighborhood volunteer, air force wives' mentor*
JEANNE EHRLICHMAN BLUECHEL	*Music program director, community leader*
SISTER MADONNA BUDER	*Nun, triathlete*
JUNE CHEN	*Teacher, systerms analyst, Seattle Taiwanese community leader*
ALICE DIETER	*Journalist, community leader for civil rights, arts, environment*
RUTH FEDER	*Teacher, volunteer director of cultural agencies*

SELMA FINK	*Teacher, artist, sculptor*
ELAINE ISHIKAWA HAYES	*Day care system developer, community leader*
JULIE HUNGAR	*Teacher, administrator, author*
EMILY KORZENIK	*Teacher, congregational rabbi, community activist*
JANET LIEBERMAN	*Professor, creator of innovative college programs, author*
RUTH LUBIC	*Pioneer founder of birthing centers, nurse midwife*
SHIRLEY MEDALIE	*Artist, jewelry designer, enamelist, volunteer*
JOYCE MILLINGTON	*Community worker, youth counselor*
JEAN PHILLIPS	*Air force officer, college dean*
"PATRICIA RADCLIFFE"	*College dean, psychologist, therapist*
MARY JANE STEVENSON	*College dean, honor society executive*
CLAUDIA THOMAS	*Teacher, administrator, mayor*
CHARLOTTE WARD	*University physics professor, volunteer*
DEBBY WING	*Teacher, college dean*
ALICE YEE	*College dean, women's right advocate, community affairs activist*

The Wisdom Trail

Introduction

The Wisdom Trail runs through the stories of the women who have lived along the fault line between two ways of defining the roles of women in the family and the wider world. Traditionally, women's principal role consisted of being a dutiful wife, the keeper of hearth and home, and the bearer and nurturer of children. Today their role includes an expectation that they will also have careers in occupations once open only to men. The women of the Wisdom Trail are now in their seventies and eighties. They first experienced the upheaval of women's roles in the twentieth century and made the transition into the new place available for women. Now, in the twenty-first, they look back and recount the events and influences, the choices and accidents that marked the paths that ultimately led to gratification and serenity.

The women we interviewed for this book are not the only ones to reach this fortunate stage. They are a sampling of the many women who have continued to have active, satisfying, useful lives far beyond the age we used to call old. They share a commitment to serving society, and they have succeeded in doing that by taking advantage of opportunities, persevering in the face of obstacles, and meeting challenges resolutely, while nurturing gratifying connections with family and friends. They are outspoken, gutsy, and undeterred by restrictive conventions. Their wisdom lies in the choices they made as the world around them changed, and in the attributes that led them to make those choices.

The women whose travels we follow have lived through extraordinary times, encompassing two different sets of expectations for women. The twists and turns of the twentieth century produced compromises and opportunities that coincided with the personal goals of the Wisdom Trail women. By seizing the possibilities inherent in prospects that appeared limited, they found growth. Their wisdom is the product of lifetimes spent embracing the challenges of their changing roles with enthusiasm.

They do not see themselves as exceptional. They were not conscious of charting a remarkable course as they did it. The Wisdom Trail is a road mapped in retrospect. The choices and characteristics that make their lives valuable as examples become apparent only when we listen to them reminisce. Like everyone in their generation, they have been shaped and buffeted by historical events, gone through the same life stages, and faced the same decisions. Yet the women of the Wisdom Trail chose to rise to the challenges, not just watch the world go by. Born and raised in a society with a definite idea of a woman's role, they were able to adapt to the changed social landscape as that role became unclear. They were ahead of the next wave, or primed to catch it as it came upon them. Most did not have a vision of what they would do, but they had an internal drive to move out of the old pattern. They seized or created opportunities to expand their lives while improving life for others. Ultimately, they left their communities, and often the wider world, a better place, and that has enriched their own lives.

For most of them, though, achievement came after

their early years and the old conventions. Girls growing up during the Great Depression and the beginning of World War II were raised with a clear, if limited, set of expectations: They would grow up to be wives and mothers, then caretakers of aging parents. Perhaps they would work before marriage in an office or a shop; they might aspire to a college education and become a schoolteacher or a nurse. The main reason for sending a girl to college at that time, though, was to find a husband, and she didn't need more than two years to do that.

This was the life pattern for most American women. Throughout our history there were a few brave pioneers who defied the conventions to become artists or writers or to enter medical or law school. There were the heroines of the women's suffrage movement, which finally bore fruit in 1920 with the passage of the Nineteenth Amendment to the Constitution, granting women the right to vote. Our women's mothers lived through the Jazz Age, when some of society's rules relaxed, but things tightened up again during the Depression.

Then World War II turned life upside down. We all know the story: Women, single and married, were needed in the workplace, even in jobs that had always been done by men, because there weren't enough men at home. Some postponed having children because their husbands were at war; others postponed marrying. Succeeding in such jobs brought a new sense of independence. Then, in the great rush to get back to normal after the war, a woman's place was back in the house, raising children and presiding over a home for the sake of her husband's career. And that's what women did; for evidence, we need look no further than the seventy-seven million baby boomers born starting in 1946 and over the next two decades. But the genie of independence had been let out of the bottle.

The women of the Wisdom Trail were born in the 1920s and 1930s, and had been nurtured on the old assumptions. Most of them married and had baby boom children. But as their children went off to school, they began to break the mold. A few of them had started careers before that; more often, the first major move outside their role as homemaker was into volunteer work. When they found they could get things done and liked what they were accomplishing, they branched out. From running a music education program as a volunteer, they might get a job on the symphony staff; from working on political campaigns, they might decide to run for office themselves.

Then the sixties blew in, and the stirring of

change grew into a wind. Already ahead of their time, our women took hold of new opportunities and raised their daughters to believe that they could do and be whatever they wanted. Many of the women of the Wisdom Trail—perhaps another aspect of their wisdom—married men who supported their aspirations and encouraged their daughters as well. The women seldom had a plan, but they were opportunists who seized openings as they appeared.

Because our women hadn't been raised with the idea that there was life beyond homemaking, few of them had even a sense that there was another goal for which they could plan. One of them described her life pattern as "zigzagging," and the description fits most of our subjects. This style has come around again, as young women are moving back and forth between working at careers and being at-home moms. But for our trailblazers, it was not a deliberate or a well-worn path.

Some would move from volunteering into teaching or nursing, careers deemed acceptable for women. Some found their way into less conventional careers like journalism, politics, or the ministry. Others joined the military or developed their creative talents. Unlike the generations growing up on this side of the divide, few Wisdom Trail women had high expectations. They enjoyed being wives and mothers, but they got bored. They wanted wider horizons, they wanted to be out in the world, and they wanted to be *useful.*

Whatever the opportunities our women found, the common ingredient was that it served the community. They discovered plenty of openings for that kind of work. Yet the divide persisted as they faced conflicting demands between their "regular jobs"— service at home—and what they chose to do outside. This was the same conflict their daughters and granddaughters face today, except that in those early days there were few models or societal norms for how to balance work inside and outside the home.

The Wisdom Trail consists not only in having lived through the long, challenging path from the twentieth to the twenty-first century. It lies in the way these women lived and the characteristics that enabled them to achieve and to continue to enjoy active and rewarding lives at an age that most didn't expect to see. Although the circumstances of their lives changed, in some ways dramatically, the attributes that allowed them to prosper when times restricted women have not diminished in value, and are as applicable today as they were fifty years ago.

Specific circumstances do create differences. Thoroughly coached to see a future that consisted of marriage-children-homemaking, these women didn't set out to break down barriers, nor did they have a specific alternative to the normal pattern in mind. Today we expect young women and men to be goal-oriented. While still in high school, they are pushed to make decisions about their future and to stay on the obligatory track toward that future. Our women's stories will hearten young people who have a hard time deciding the future shape of their lives. The stories of those who followed the Wisdom Trail support the modern model that promotes entrepreneurial skills and includes the likelihood of having several different careers.

One theme of our women's lives is that it's possible to do very well without a definite life plan. But while our women didn't have a plan, they got an education, which was essential. It might not have been in a subject they pursued later in life, but it was a necessary launching platform. Many of those on the Wisdom Trail enjoyed social and economic advantages not shared by all Americans, while others lived in poverty during the Depression. They all shared, though, in the broad benefits that came with the expansion of the middle class after World War II. Almost every one of them graduated from college, which put them in the minority for their generation. But they all struggled to make their way against the tide of social convention. That was easier for some than for others, depending on where their journey began.

Wisdom Trail women exemplify the best of their generation. They thrived through each stage of the transformation of women's role in society. These women are not a statistically valid sample, nor do they represent the many spheres in which women are now active. In other ways they are typical of their generation. Like the great majority of their peers, most of them married and had children. Some are widows and divorcees; a few never married. Some of them knew poverty as they were growing up, and some would be considered middle class today. Many worked in education, from elementary school to university, as teachers, counselors, or administrators. Others made their marks in politics, health, or the arts. Since one of the authors is from the East Coast and one is from the West, most of our women are from the coasts, but the South and the Midwest are represented too. Those who are religious are Christian or Jewish. Most are Caucasian, but there are African Americans and Asian Americans here as well. Two are immigrants. The group ranges in age from seventy-three to ninety.

We, the authors, have walked the Wisdom Trail and are members of this group. Janet was born in 1921 and Julie in 1931. We wrote this book because very little has been written about the widespread and significant accomplishments of more or less average women of our generation. We looked at the women we knew or knew of and identified those we admired. As we've said, they shared a commitment to serving others. We sought women who had made a real difference, whose lives are ordinary and yet exemplary, and whose achievements have brought them contentment and wisdom. Their stories are recounted memories, many of them from times long past. The chronology may not always be accurate. The reminiscences may differ from others' memories of those times. Irregularities, inherent in the fabric of memory, matter little here, where the value lies in the meaning these women draw from the past as they reflect on it in the present.

SEVERAL QUALITIES make Wisdom Trail women special. First is adaptability when confronting a constricting system. It's the ability to worm their way around or through constraints that seem impenetrable to direct attack. Our women saw that to do what they wanted to do they had to find ways to adapt to the rules while keeping their sanity, keeping their hopes up, and keeping their options open. Charlotte Ward honed this skill as the only woman chemistry major in her university in the late 1940s. Her adviser, the chair of the department, did not believe in having women in his department. She says, "I would take a deep breath and prepare to go in each quarter and listen to his little talk on how I should consider becoming a chemical secretary or a librarian. I would smile and try to look pleasant, get his signature, then I went on and majored in chemistry." It was a time and place when arguing was counterproductive, so she didn't; she adapted, and went on to earn a doctorate and become a university professor.

As young wives, if the women of the Wisdom Trail needed to get out of the house and there wasn't money to spare, they traded babysitting duties with neighbors. If taking a paying job outside the home wasn't an option, they found volunteer work that didn't interfere too much—in the beginning, at least—with household and child-raising duties. They were pragmatic; they recognized their limitations and lived within them, but they learned to make accommodations that enabled them to maintain their home lives and explore beyond their own backyards.

Ruth Lubic is a prime example. To found and operate the nation's first birthing centers staffed by nurse-midwives, she learned how to enlist allies in challenging powerful opposition. She adapted her approach to each potential donor to steer her centers through near-fatal financial straits. Janet Lieberman employed the same skill and political savvy in developing award-winning projects at LaGuardia Community College in Queens. Weaving her way through the treacherous ins and outs of New York's educational system, she created lasting programs that improved educational opportunities for underserved students.

Adapting to the life of a service wife during and after World War II had its own requirements, and Nell Berry is representative of the many women who walked this path on the Wisdom Trail. She and her Air Force officer husband had two children and moved twenty-two times during his service career, which ended with his death in a test flight. During their twenty-five-year marriage, Nell's husband was often stationed abroad. In those times, she had sole responsibility for raising the children and taking care of the household, managing each move, and making new friends while keeping in touch with old ones. She also carried out the duties of an officer's wife at a time when those duties played a significant part in an officer's advancement. Nell believes she and her children adapted well to this life. Adjusting was much more difficult after her husband was killed, but Nell says, "We coped."

Another attribute of the Wisdom Trail women is improvisation. These women seized the day, even if they did not advertise it or admit it to themselves. It was important—it still is, in fact—for women not to appear too ambitious. Our women had to latch on to opportunities that fit their need to stretch. They became volunteers and made themselves indispensable, so they were later taken on for pay. They took entry-level jobs and worked harder and faster, and so gained advancement. They built up women's organizations to wield political power. They offered classes in their basements or worked on their art at home and found commercial outlets elsewhere. They improvised avenues to community service and personal enrichment without neglecting or abandoning their families.

Alice Dieter's start came when she got angry. She was a Boise, Idaho, housewife at home minding her one-year-old when she got a telephone call inviting her to subscribe to a new weekly newspaper that "aimed at the intelligent part of the community." She took it. Then the first copy came and she was incensed, she remembers, "because they had just added a women's page and anchored it with Heloise's Household Hints."

She pulled out her old typewriter and listed twenty-five Boise women who would make better copy than Heloise and her hints, wrote a story about one of them, "stalked into the editor's office, and slammed it down on his desk." The editor asked her for more, then started paying her two dollars apiece, and she was hooked. So began Alice's long career in print and broadcast journalism, in which she made her mark as a liberal voice in her conservative city. And she was able to do most of her work at home while her children were small.

Perseverance was another vital characteristic of the Wisdom Trail women. They faced plenty of obstacles, but they refused to accept discouragement. They looked for alternative routes when the direct way was blocked. When they found what they wanted to pursue, they stuck with it and found ways to make their goals fit into the limitations of their world.

As a young mother of three, including one in a bassinet, Emily Korzenik was taking action in her community. She began by raising money for the presidential campaign of Adlai Stevenson, a tough task in her conservative suburb. Then she campaigned for election to her town's governing board, trying to open up a closed, elitist system. She lost the election, but she was encouraged; her campaign spurred many more citizens to vote. She then ran for the New York State Assembly.

Again, she lost, but, she says, "It was great fun. I picked issues I wanted to talk about." Her persistence came into play again when she decided to go to rabbinical school to use her leadership skills in another arena.

Julie Hungar's mother always urged her to get a teaching certificate, but that didn't appeal to Julie until she volunteered in her children's classrooms. She realized that she would rather be in charge of the class and decided to pursue teaching college students. With only one year of teaching experience, she couldn't even get an interview when she applied for a position at Seattle Central Community College. To get her foot in the door, she went back to school for a teaching certificate in order to do her practice teaching at the college. First she had to persuade her university adviser that this would be valid experience for someone seeking a certificate to teach high school; then she had to persuade a college professor to accept her as an intern. Once in the door, she was offered a part-time job; when a full-time position opened, she got the job and was on her way to a fruitful career.

Courage is another quality that enabled our Wisdom Trail women to make risky personal career decisions and to speak truth to power. They have faced down racial and gender bias in hiring and housing, and they have battled bureaucracies to improve health care and educational opportunities. It has helped them through experiences as devastating as the death of or estrangement from a child, or the death of a young husband and father, or a marriage that ends in divorce. It's a quality none of them would claim for herself, but it comes through clearly in their matter-of-fact ways of describing difficult events.

Claudia Thomas is mayor of Lakewood, Washington, a city of nearly sixty thousand next to the army's Fort Lewis. As an African American, she is a pioneer, but before she was an elected official, she was a teacher. In that role she sued her school district over their failure to hire not African Americans, but women, after the district administrator summarily rejected her application for a vice principal position. It was not her first challenge nor her last.

It took another kind of courage for Jeanne Bluechel, a stay-at-home mom, to stand up to Antal Doráti, the famous conductor of the Washington, D.C., symphony. As a new member of the symphony board, she insisted that children from the city, most of whom were black, should be included with those from the suburbs in the symphony's concerts for children. She provided educational materials to prepare the D.C. fourth-graders for the concert, and afterward Doráti generously admitted the audience was one of the best. The program Jeanne started continued for many years.

While the women of the Wisdom Trail were each broadening their lives beyond the limiting conventions of the times in which they lived, they never lost touch with the deep satisfactions of being a woman. All of them possess the capacity to form and sustain deeply satisfying relationships with their families, friends, and fellow strivers. They consistently look beyond themselves to care for others at an individual and a community level. Their husbands were at least accepting, and at best supportive, of their wives' efforts. In her native Trinidad, Joyce Millington carried on what she calls her "social work," following the example of her mother. Whenever Joyce saw people in need, especially children, she found ways to help them. Knowing her husband's extremely thrifty nature, she wouldn't tell him she was buying extra groceries for a family she knew was going hungry. But she knew he would never criticize her if he found out.

Most of our women had children, and when they are asked to reflect on what is most important in their lives, they say it is their families, the children and grandchildren that give them joy and anguish. Alice Yee struggled to protect her three children, who ranged in age from nine to seventeen, from some of the grief she was feeling as their father, her first husband, was dying of Hodgkin's disease. She kept him at home as long as possible, because they knew that once he went into the hospital, he would not return. During his last two and a half months, she took her children to see him only when he was having a good day and could sit up and talk to them. "The memories they have are not mine," she says, because she was there on the bad days as well.

All Shirley Medalie ever wanted to be was a mother. She married a young naval officer a year before World War II ended, and she and her husband had a daughter and a son, but her mothering was never limited to her own children. A few years ago she had a flash of self-awareness when she read a letter Albert Einstein had written to a woman whose child had died. It included this line: "Our task must be to free ourselves from this prison of separateness by widening our circle of compassion to embrace all living creatures and all nature and its beauty." She says, "As my grandchildren got older and lived farther away from me, I began adopting other people. Actually, I've adopted people all my life, but I didn't know I was doing it until I read Einstein's letter." Some of her most gratifying "adop-

tions" are of patients she volunteers to help in art therapy classes at a New York hospital.

The women who never married found other
avenues to strong, caring relationships. A number of
members of the Peaceful Valley Group, composed of
deans from liberal arts colleges throughout the country, remained single all their lives. The group initially
came together because of common professional interests. At their first meeting in a rustic Colorado retreat,
they realized how valuable the exchange of ideas was
for their work, so they decided to meet again. Over
the course of the next forty years, their annual week-
long meeting grew into a source of deep comradeship
and support that has been one of the most important
aspects of their lives.

The capstone characteristic of all Wisdom Trail
women is a lifetime commitment to serving the community and the world beyond. Each of them has made
her mark and gained gratification by making a difference. All of them have followed a path of working to
solve community problems. It has kept them going
long after most people their age retire, and has been a
source of deep satisfaction.

The aggregate of attributes provided a foundation
for the life choices of those who walked the Wisdom

Trail. Many others have traveled this road, each on her own journey. The routes taken by the women whose lives are recounted here show that there are many possibilities for forging a well-lived life, and many opportunities to seize and act on with courage, flexibility, perseverance, and love.

ONE

The Hinge Generation Comes of Age

The women who traveled from adolescence into young womanhood during and after World War II couldn't know it at the time, but they were going to traverse a new terrain. The conventions that shaped their early lives were deeply ingrained in the fabric of society. Whether rich or poor, urban or rural, immigrant or native born, families held common ideas of what it meant to be a woman. Admired and praised for "keeping their looks" while bearing and raising children, cooking, and instilling moral values, women were not supposed to play an active role outside the home. Although they gained the right to vote in 1920, women's place in public life nevertheless remained largely the same as before that milestone.

Families are vital carriers of social conventions, most effectively in a child's early years. During the decades of the twenties and thirties, the values and intentions of families and the society at large were compatible. The women of the Wisdom Trail were firmly grounded in the norms of their time, even those who came from less traditional families. Early on, a few of them had a sense of a future that went beyond the normal horizon, but they all understood the expectations, and nearly all fulfilled them.

As they were growing into adulthood, though, the society around them was opening up. In the 1940s, Rosie the Riveter became the symbol of the woman who showed her patriotism by taking a man's job to help the war effort. In hindsight, this phenomenon would be seen as instrumental in enabling women to move into the economic and educational mainstream. But at the time, a return to normal life appeared to follow the war and characterize the fifties. But over the next two decades, a shift occurred, and the repercussions of women entering the workforce were finally felt. Having grown up under the influence of the old rules, the women of the Wisdom Trail were poised to become pioneers in the shift from the restrictive con-

ventions of their upbringing to the broader expectations of the future.

What made these women able to change with the
times? Part of the explanation lay with their families, but family influences varied. Those who grew up
in small towns experienced different influences from
those who lived in the city. Their place in the family
had an effect, as did whether or not they were raised
by two parents. In recalling their childhood and teenage years, the women of the Wisdom Trail cite specific
elements that influenced their later lives. They seldom
connect family influence with their later accomplishments. Still, it is possible to see connections between
how they were brought up and who they became.

The families of most of these women were typical
of the time, with a mother and a father and at least two
children, and with the usual ideas of what the future
would hold for their girls. But the fact that girls' lives
were considered set and didn't need special shaping
gave each of them a measure of freedom she was able
to act on when the opportunity came to expand and
break the mold.

Alice Yee learned about hard work and making
the best of things from the way her mother managed
during the Depression, when Alice's father was out of
work. She remembers that her mother didn't push her

children, but if they had an idea and it wasn't too outrageous, she always said, "Go ahead and try it." As a child of immigrant parents, Lorraine Beitler imbibed two important lessons: first, gratitude for the opportunity to learn, and second, the absolute necessity to excel in school. She did excel, but it was her brother who got the attention.

Other girls had less conventional upbringings. Charlotte Ward was raised by three great-aunts and a great-uncle. The uncle shared his love of learning with her, and by the time she was in eighth grade she had decided to be a college professor. This makes her unusual among our group in identifying the direction her life would take at an early age. Ruth Lubic grew up working in her family's pharmacy; her father died when she was fourteen, and she and her mother continued to run it alone. Claudia Thomas also worked alongside her mother, who ran their town's general store. She developed a strong taste for independence that carried her through several careers.

For the women of the Wisdom Trail, nothing was expected, though much was possible. Reflecting the emerging importance of college, they got an education and usually married. Along the way they developed the confidence and courage that prepared them to move out into the world and surmount the barriers that defeated other women of their generation.

Education was certainly one key to their success. In the 1930s, parents began to recognize the value of education as a way out of poverty, and the number of teenagers attending high school increased significantly. High school graduation was generally the highest expectation for girls, but many parents aspired to a college education for their daughters as well as their sons. Although the explicit purpose of sending a girl to college might be to help her find a promising husband—the joke was that you went to college to get an Mrs. degree—the Wisdom Trail women liked learning and sought an education. Most earned degrees, and a number went on to even higher education. Some were encouraged by their parents, but others, from families who thought college was unnecessary for girls, made the decision on their own. Education set all of them up for future accomplishments. They had the credentials and the knowledge to launch themselves when they were ready.

Another key was hard work, a consistent weapon in the arsenal of family values. It surely played a part in developing the perseverance that enabled Wisdom Trail women to overcome obstacles. Lorraine Beitler is a good example. Her parents had emigrated from Russia, she says, "looking for all the values America spoke of." Her mother came from a fairly comfortable life in Russia, but when her family sent her to this country she had to work hard. Lorraine's father's family were well respected but poor. At sixteen, he was forced to join the Russian army, was nearly killed, and eventually escaped. Later he emigrated to America, where he met and married her mother. Lorraine says her parents were very grateful to be in this country: "You could work, and nobody could abuse you, and nobody would police you, and nobody would beat you or cut your head off just because they felt like it."

Lorraine's parents considered it a great privilege to be able to send their children to school for free; her mother thought that meant her children had earned scholarships. If Lorraine got a 95 on a test, her mother would ask, "What happened to the other five points?" Lorraine remembers her weekly test well: "Every Friday morning I'd throw up my breakfast because I was so nervous about losing those five points. There was a lot of tension, because my parents thought I'd lose my scholarship, and then I wouldn't be able to go to school anymore." Others might have buckled, but Lorraine did very well. She skipped a grade in elementary school and, at seventeen, entered college, the first person in her family to do so. She felt even more pressure to prove herself there. She chose chemistry: "I had to have a job when I got out, and I had to prove that I was worthy, that the years I spent in school were a meaningful sacrifice for my parents."

While Lorraine was working hard to make sure she did not disappoint her parents, she was also to some extent the head of the household. She was the eldest and spoke English well. She took care of things that she could do better than her parents, such as paying the bills, because she knew more about navigating life in the United States. She accepted her position, grateful, as she says, "that my parents were brave enough to come to this country. We avoided the Holocaust. I felt very protective and grateful that they came here, because they provided us with a future. I was never resentful or thought that I should have more or less. Whatever we had was a gift." Her dual responsibilities helped Lorraine develop the confidence, compassion, and courage that would mark the path of her life.

That path has carried her to accomplishments in education, finance, and the ethics of military justice. In her eighties now, she looks much younger and is in constant motion. Though she is self-deprecating about her achievements, she is passionate about the causes she serves, and her zeal is enlivened by a sense of humor.

Hard work is a constant theme running through the lives of most Americans who lived through the Depression. Hard work in hard times surely contributed to the strength and staying power of Wisdom Trail women who remember difficult early days. From the vantage point of their lives today, which are comfortable and filled with the pleasure of accomplishment, they look at those early years with equanimity. It's just the way things were, as they see it, and things turned out well after all.

Alice Yee's memories of childhood are good, despite the poverty that overtook her family during the thirties: "Things were pretty rough. My parents really had no money, but we never felt deprived. We managed, because my folks were very frugal."

This is typical of Alice's positive attitude. She is frank about the crises and sadness in her life, but she prefers to emphasize her good fortune. She believes that many of her opportunities were simply the result of luck. She is tall and slender, serene and gracious, self-contained but warm. She is computer-literate in her eighties and has thoroughly modern views. She works to preserve the environment; is an active supporter of women's rights; and is comfortable in her satisfying second marriage.

Until Alice was in elementary school, her father,

who was a butcher, had his own meat market. "We had wonderful food," she says, "but it was all leftovers, everything that wouldn't sell. So we learned to like all the parts of an animal that nobody else wanted—the brains and the heart and the kidney." Her mother, who had only an eighth-grade education, was good with figures and had been a bookkeeper before she was married—an old-maid bookkeeper, since she didn't marry Alice's father until the ripe old age of thirty. She kept the books for the meat market, and tried to tell her husband that his partner was cheating him, but he didn't believe her until they went broke. The family, including four children, moved to another town, where he found work for a while. Then he lost that job and they moved again. He wound up working for the Works Progress Administration—one of the Roosevelt administration's projects to provide jobs—making the handsome sum of fifty-five dollars a month.

Still, Alice says, "we managed—my mother managed. She made all of our clothes. In the early years we had a big washboard to wash clothes, and we hung them on the line outside. Then we graduated to a washing machine with a ringer you turned. We did canning—we picked berries in season, and my mother made jam. We picked beans, squash, corn. It was not unusual for us to have several hundred quarts of canned fruit and vegetables in the cellar. We never lacked for food."

Alice and her siblings had fun, too. When she and her two sisters and her brother all had smallpox and were quarantined, they spent almost a week building a miniature golf course, using whatever materials they could find. "When the kids across the street came home from school, they lined up on the road watching us play miniature golf, and they all wished they had smallpox, too, so they wouldn't have to go to school. Kids created their own fun. We didn't have money, but that didn't keep us from being creative or doing what we wanted to do." She thinks that perhaps the reason they never felt deprived was that everyone they knew was in the same boat. The self-reliance and creativity released by feeling free to seize the opportunity at hand may be a special legacy of those Depression years, a gift from parents who were able to keep themselves and their children from being ground down by poverty.

Poverty and hard work were also factors in the life of Jeanne Ehrlichman Bluechel, and helped her develop the strength with which she has navigated the high and low points in her story. But other factors in her childhood were also integral to her outlook. She was an only child whose parents divorced when she was eight years old. Divorce was not common then; it was at best an embarrassment, certainly a disgrace, and at worst a sin. Jeanne adored her father, and until he remarried she saw him every week, going on hikes or ice-skating. But she lived with her mother until she graduated from college and got married. They were always poor. Her mother never owned a car; she made all Jeanne's clothes; they lived in rented apartments and shared their only bed. Jeanne occasionally visited her father and his new family, and she was aware of the difference between the warm and respectable family life that her half brother and sister lived, and the spare apartment where she and her mother lived.

The worst part was her mother's anger. She was always fighting with someone, and Jeanne was never sure what would trigger her rage. Often it was directed at Jeanne. If they went to the home of one of her mother's brothers for a holiday, the anger would be directed at him; Jeanne had to be careful not to be too nice to her uncles, or she would be in trouble when she got home. Likewise, when she came home from visiting her dad and his second family, her mother would be mad if Jeanne let on that she'd had a good time.

But her mother loved music, and somehow found

money for piano lessons and tickets and bus fare to take Jeanne to hear the Los Angeles Symphony. Jeanne coped with her mother's temperament by spending every available minute practicing the piano. It kept Jeanne out of her mother's way and kept her mother in relatively good spirits. As Jeanne sees it, "Music saved my life." Jeanne became an excellent pianist, and gave recitals and performed at school through junior high and high school.

Jeanne is very clear about her mother's legacy. First, she is grateful for the gift of music. Second, she still carries the determination to be nice to everyone, to be the opposite of her mother. The discipline required to avoid or suppress anger may have come at a cost, but it enabled her to weather some stormy times and to have a benevolent influence in her community.

She decided early that she would have lots of children, and today she has close and loving—though not clinging—relationships with her large family. Her toughness is all inside. On the surface she is warm, charming, and indefatigably upbeat. Small, feminine, and energetic, she works continually to promote the issues that engage her enthusiasm. At the same time, she is solicitous of the needs and feelings of others, and generous and encouraging.

A different family constellation fostered Janet Lieberman's confidence. Coming from a middle-class Jewish family, in which first sons are the cherished children, she found freedom in being a second child and a girl. In families like hers, she says, "where there was an older male child, he was the prince of the family. The first-born male child in the Jewish family at that time was the center of attention, and his progress was highly important. In my case that was very beneficial. I profited from being neglected: Nobody expected anything of me, and whatever I did was considered marvelous. There was no standard to live up to." Early in childhood she understood that a seeming negative could, in fact, be positive. This insight left her free to "fly under the radar," as she recalls. She was able to experiment with ideas and create a path for herself that carried the values of her family into a broader arena.

Janet's mother was a significant influence in her upbringing. "She was the most active parent, and she was also an unstated role model. My father was sweet and quietly loving. I could do no wrong as far as he was concerned, and I never gave anyone any trouble. I profited from benign neglect, which gave me a wide choice of activities. I didn't have any encouragement, but I didn't have any discouragement either. My mother's idea was that I would grow up and play canasta."

A life of card playing, however, was definitely not what Janet had in mind. She loved learning and going to school. It was easy for her, and pleasant, it provided a lot of satisfaction and rewards, and when she grew up she found teaching as well as learning very satisfying. Helping others who were less privileged was a significant value in her family, one she would later express by working to give others the same benefits she had gotten from education. The confidence she gained from charting her own course gave her the courage to confront entrenched systems.

Creativity is another of Janet's signature qualities. In her late eighties, she is still thinking about how to improve education for students who have been undervalued and underserved by our system, and she continues to enlist her vast contacts in education in support of her latest project. She always has time to mentor and nurture promising young people, passing on her lifelong passion for education.

For Alice Dieter, freedom and confidence came from being the apple of her parents' eyes. They lived on a farm and were "dirt poor. As people used to say, we had lots of dirt and nobody was buying it. So it was a pretty hardscrabble time. But I grew up never hungry; we were outstanding in the community in that we had indoor plumbing." Her father, who ran away from home at fifteen, had not finished high school. He ended up in Denver, took adult high school classes, and wooed and married his mathematics teacher.

Alice's mother came from a very privileged family. She had graduated from Wellesley in math, and was a teacher until her marriage. So Alice inhabited two different worlds. One was the farm and the country town where she went to school, "with kids whose parents were immigrants, and who were living in basement houses that they hadn't built a first floor on yet." Then she would go to the Denver Country Club as the guest of her mother's friends' children, and "we'd have cocoa and they'd ring the bell for the maid." "I was in and out of these worlds and never totally part of anything. At the time it seemed hard to me. In every case I was just a little outside, observing it and wanting to be integrated. When I joined the Girl Scouts I felt that was wonderful."

When she grew up, Alice's desire to be part of a group started her on a path of activism that began when she joined the League of Women Voters. It appealed to a value passed down by her parents: the importance of being involved in the community. Her activism, including leadership in the women's movement in Idaho, reflects their example. If there was a problem in her community, her father tried to deal with it. People came to him for advice and help when they were in trouble. He once organized a successful campaign to force the Union Pacific Railroad to install a crossing signal in their town. Her mother, who had earned a master's degree after her marriage, was elected to the school board, and she battled other members who didn't want to hire teachers with degrees because they would be "uppity." She eventually traveled around the West interviewing for the Elmo Roper polls, which helped put food on the family's table during the Depression.

Alice recalls her childhood as idyllic. She and her parents were like the Three Musketeers. From her mother came "a great love of learning and determination for education." She admires her parents and they have been powerful role models for her commitment to make a difference in the community and her courage and persistence in tackling obstacles. Alice has exploited the values they gave her in campaigns to promote open space, civil rights, international awareness, and cultural development in her community. They have also helped her through personal tragedy. Her view of the world is humorous and perceptive, and she is not afraid to state her opinions.

. . .

MANY WOMEN OF the Wisdom Trail were fortunate in having mothers who were admirable role models within the limits of their conventional roles. They worked hard, didn't let hard times wear them down, adapted to their circumstances, and gave their children love and the freedom and confidence to experiment. The message of self-reliance and self-confidence was even more powerful when a mother had broken through traditional boundaries and carved out a role for herself that was courageous for its time. Claudia Thomas had such a mother. She had a general store, the biggest business in her North Carolina town. Claudia's father died when she was three years old, and her mother ran the business on her own. Her father, Claudia's grandfather, came to live with them, and he became the male figure in their life.

"My real passion for people came through my mother's example as a businesswoman," Claudia says. "As I look at life today, I see my mother was long before her time. She was thinking and doing things that people are just now doing." The store sold food, clothes, and gasoline. It had space for dancing, and on weekends people would come and play the jukebox and dance.

They lived in a "white" neighborhood; the nearest black neighbors were a quarter of a mile away. The town had a mixed Indian, caucasian, and black population. Claudia's heritage is Indian, Scotch, and African American. People often tell her, "You seem comfortable in your own skin," and she explains that her mother taught her that "people are people no matter what color they are, and it's the behavior of people you have to be concerned with, not their color. My mother didn't let us think any other way."

Claudia's mother fought for what she believed in. She argued at the state capital to have the school district lines redrawn so that her children could attend a city school. She succeeded. Although Claudia went to all-black schools, they were superior to those in the country. Her mother was also a role model for her involvement in the community. In addition to the store, she owned a farm, and when she found that the lunches in the black schools didn't provide a balanced diet, she sent food from her store and her farm to provide healthy meals for the children. Given her mother's legacy, it is not surprising that Claudia would one day become one of the first black mayors of a city in Washington State.

Claudia is matter-of-fact about what she has done. But with the confidence that comes from having been her grandfather's favorite, and benefiting from her mother's life and wisdom, her presence is authoritative and she exudes competence and a solid sense of her priorities. She is direct but cordial, comfortable with herself and accepting of others.

Three women of the Wisdom Trail who have been heavily involved with politics were raised by mothers who had what even today would be considered real careers. Like Claudia Thomas and Alice Dieter, Ruth Lubic was raised by a woman who was successful in business. Ruth has been engaged with the political system at state and national levels for over thirty years, battling for the birth centers she founded. Her family experiences and the example her parents set were precursors to her independence and commitment to service, and explain the contribution she is making to the health and well-being of women and infants.

Ruth has a passion for poor mothers and their babies. In her early eighties, she still works to ameliorate their plight with youthful energy and ardor. She is articulate about her agenda and her anger at those in positions to help who don't see their responsibilities. But she is wise in wielding her strength; she keeps her anger to herself when she approaches bureaucrats, politicians, or grant-making officers whose help she is seeking. She is warm, but she doesn't sentimentalize her work or her clients.

In her childhood in a Pennsylvania town, "Our drugstore dominated our lives." Her father and mother kept it open from 9:00 A.M. until 10:00 P.M. during the week, until 11:00 P.M. on Saturdays, and from 9:00 to 1:00 and 6:00 until 10:00 on Sundays. Her parents, Ruth, and her older sister only had Sunday afternoon together. Neither parent went to church, but her father's family was quite religious, so Ruth went to the Baptist church with her father's mother and his sister, Marie. "Fun was having the preacher in for Sunday dinner. Aunt Marie did not play cards or wear lipstick. It was the old Baptist tough line." When Ruth learned the meaning of full-immersion baptism, she opted out, to her aunt's disappointment. Later, after the birth of their son, she and her husband became Unitarians.

She remembers the Great Depression, and the things her family did to help people in poverty. "I always knew you spent long hours working and were friendly with the customers that came in. You knew a lot about them, and they knew a lot about you. So I grew up thinking that you should really help people who were less fortunate than you were." Their generosity is symbolized by the story of her mother's diamond ring, which she wears today. When money was especially tight, the ring was the family's only source of cash for buying medicine for people in town who couldn't afford to buy it themselves. Since their town of thirteen thousand didn't have a pawnshop, among Ruth's earliest memories are trips to Philadelphia to get the ring out of hock.

Her father died in January 1942, just after the war started. Ruth was fourteen. "I suppose my mother could have thrown in the towel, but she kept the store open. In Pennsylvania you could operate without a pharmacist. Everybody was being drafted, and she couldn't find one to work there. I helped her." Ruth's sister was away at the state teachers college, so she and her mother were on their own. Ruth would eat dinner at the Keystone Hotel and take food to her mother at the pharmacy. In the hotel dining room she became acquainted with a new young doctor in the town who encouraged her to go into nursing. His advice helped set the course of her life, but she didn't follow it right away. She graduated at the top of her high school class, but her mother needed her in the store, so she decided not to go to college. It would be seven years before she went back to school.

She had thought about going to medical school, because her father had wanted to become a doctor, but had been forced to drop out and take care of his father's pharmacy when his father died. Her mother had wanted Ruth to be a pharmacist, but her father had said, "It's no life for a woman, Ruth. Don't do it. You do what you want to do." When Ruth found out how much medical school cost, and how little it cost to go to nursing school, she decided to follow the advice of her friend, the doctor. She ran the pharmacy by herself to make the money she needed to train as a nurse.

The significance of education for the generation of the Wisdom Trail is difficult to overestimate. Knowing that they could master a discipline or profession built confidence. Competing with men successfully to earn the credentials that gave them entrée into the man's world was a higher order of validation. In the 1940s and 1950s just attending college had to give girls a sense that they were special; in 1950, not quite one third of college students were women. Today women are in the majority in higher education, but in those days they were the exception, and it gave them higher expectations of themselves.

Wisdom Trail women used their college education as a launching pad, whether they took off right after college or, like most of their educated peers, took the route of "family then job." Charlotte Ward went directly toward her goal, following the same path as women today who are trying to have it all, all at the same time. She exhibited a key element of wisdom: She married a man who was supportive of her goal, shared her academic interests, and understood what she was trying to achieve.

Shortly after Charlotte was born, her mother died of an infection that might have been cured had sulfa drugs been available at the time. Her father disappeared from her life for most of her childhood, leaving her in the charge of the three maiden great-aunts and the bachelor great-uncle. "He was the great influence in my life. He taught me about nature and baseball and politics, and what else does a girl need to know? My earliest memories are of his taking me for walks, telling me the names of flowers, trees, and birds, looking at stars and identifying constellations. I wonder if that was my initial introduction to an interest in science."

The aunts had to make their own living, and worked at the local department store. They were caretakers for the whole family, including various cousins, nieces, and nephews, and an uncle, the black sheep of the family, who had been paralyzed from drinking bad liquor during Prohibition. Charlotte "always felt kind of sorry for kids who just had parents. I was so spoiled, it's a wonder I learned to tie my own shoes." In fact, her middle aunt, Emma, read Charlotte's lessons to her while Charlotte sat on a footstool (it's in her bedroom now) and drew paper dolls. "This was a marvelous habit to have acquired when I got to college—I was used to learning through my ears, so the lecture system presented no problems to me. I don't know how many people passed their analytic chemistry qualifying exam at Purdue on my lecture notes."

Charlotte recalls a wonderful childhood. She didn't have many playmates her own age, but she had a wonderful imagination. Her great interest in high school was history, but she also took general chemistry, which was taught by the high school football and basketball coach, "a gentleman by the name of Tiny Jones in deference to his three-hundred-pound weight." The athletes took his course because he saw to it that they passed. He would stand by the desk of one of his players during the test and say, "You know the answer to that, Eddie. It's four letters, starts with an A." When Charlotte was in his homeroom, he regularly announced to the class that the only reason she had good grades was because the women teachers gave her As. He promised that she would get her comeuppance when she took his chemistry class. "I used to cry all the way home at lunch out of fury. I thought I'd show him if it killed me."

Of course, she did show him, and he wound up urging her to major in chemistry, but she had her mind set on history. That was her major when she started college at sixteen, but she also signed up for a chemistry course. She was in a class full of chemistry majors, and breezed through it. By the end of the first term the chemistry professor, too, was urging her to major in it, and when she got an A in chemistry and a B in history she saw the wisdom of his advice. That's how Charlotte found her true direction, and later her husband as well. Ultimately they both became university professors, but not until they had earned doctorates and started a family.

She and her husband never owned a car. Once they finished college, their life was spent in a college town, Auburn, Alabama, and they got along fine without driving. Blessed with a colorful Kentucky-spawned sense of humor most often directed at herself, Charlotte is amusing about being known in her community as "the Bicycle Lady." She is good company—interesting and wise, warm and unintimidating.

Charlotte Ward found her way early, but she is not typical of the women of the Wisdom Trail. Most of them took a circuitous route, circling back to college when they found an opening or a clear direction. Their stories prove that taking time to find the main road is not a bad thing. For women of whom little was expected, it is not surprising that they would take a while to find their way.

Although the Wisdom Trail eventually led Emily Korzenik to a career as a rabbi, she made plenty of satisfying turns en route. She feels that her life has been tremendously blessed, starting with the family she was born into, which, as she says, "you have nothing to do with." She had all the advantages of having parents who adore their children and who gave her a good sense of herself as an American and as a Jew. Her mother saw to it that she had a solid grounding in her religion; Hebrew school gave her a close group of friends as well.

Learning was an integral part of her family's life. Her mother had been an elementary school teacher, so Emily was her guinea pig. "When she was making my bottle curls in the morning, she had me practice the multiplication tables," she says. "So I was a star in mathematics because I knew it cold. It was a Jewish family, so what did we do at the dinner table? We were given mathematics problems. We thought that was fun. And if we did well and were praised for it, that was fun."

She went to a public elementary school, then her parents sent her to a private high school because they thought she would have a better chance of going to a good college if she came from a private school, which at the time didn't have as many Jewish students. Her parents were aware that most colleges had a strict quota on the number of Jewish students they would accept. Her high school was all girls for her first two years; then it merged with a coeducational school, and she had a chance to see how different that was. For one thing, the students were much less boisterous and better mannered in the girls' school. More important, though, in the all-girls school everyone spoke up and girls were editors of the newspaper and presidents of the class and had all the leadership opportunities. "The point is that the girls who merged and still had some classes together, we all spoke up, and the girls from the coed classes did not. It was a whole different atmosphere in terms of what we expected of ourselves. We were talking and raising our hands, but for the most part the girls in the coed groups were not."

Emily was remarkably mature, a quality her high school teachers commented on, as a result of circumstances at home. Despite her parents' lively and public social life, they did not have a happy marriage. Her father once told her, "If it weren't for you children I wouldn't be here." Emily saw that in a positive light; she felt it showed his dedication to his responsibilities as well as a deep affection for his children. She saw that in her mother, too. Still, their relationship created a burden for Emily. Her brother had left for college when she was twelve, and she was alone in the middle of her parents' bickering. She became the confidante of each of them, a difficult position for a young girl. She recalls that at summer camp, "I was always the one in the bunk that put the kid who had problems to bed and hugged her and kissed her." She sums up that aspect of her family life today: "Sweet are the uses of adversity."

When it came time for college, Emily was fortunate to be able to go to Vassar, which was then for women only. She decided to major in economics because she thought it would increase her understanding of the world, and she could still use her skill in math. The economics faculty was superb. "There was one rootin' tootin' dame after another." Beyond the academics, they instilled high expectations in their students. One professor told her class, "I want you to understand that you have a responsibility to your community. You are privileged to be here and to get what you're getting, so when you leave here you must keep that in mind. Do not come back to me after your two adorable little children are in high school and tell me you are playing bridge. And don't ask me what you should do with the rest of your life. You should be planning it *now*!"

Even Vassar girls, though, were being groomed for marriage. "I was being educated to be a proper wife to an intellectual, professional man. Another primary role of our education was to see that our children were educated properly, and we were going to be the primary people responsible."

In her family and her professional life, Emily internalized the charge her professors gave their students. She has an unusual appreciation for her good fortune and for what she has accomplished. Her experience has given her self-esteem, her ability for reflection, self-awareness. She shares herself with candor, and has a manner of equanimity that is reassuring.

THE TIMETABLE WAS different for our women of the "hinge generation" who never married. Unlike those who followed the more common path— marrying, having children, then expanding into the wider world—single women didn't have that luxury. They started working young and they kept working because they had to support themselves. Many of them drifted into a single life, but they also drifted into professions in which they could help people while making a living. Their careers also offered them rewarding relationships. Most of them look back with satisfaction and without regret at the choices they made.

Sister Madonna Buder is one of the few women of the Wisdom Trail who decided early on—when she was fourteen—what she would do with her life. It definitely did not include marriage. Inspired by a Catholic nun who helped her when she entered a new school in the seventh grade, she determined that she would become a nun. Although her mother was a good Catholic, she tried to talk her daughter out of it. Marie (her name before she entered the order) decided she would do what her mother wanted until she grew up. Through high school and college she was a social butterfly, enjoying parties and a string of beaus. She majored in education, and after college taught first grade for a year. Then she surprised her social circle by following her long-held intention and entering the convent of the Sisters of the Good Shepherd.

The work of her order was providing homes for girls who had been committed to the sisters' care by the courts. Sister Madonna had empathy for them and was dedicated to "taking care of these girls around the clock, trying to reeducate them and make them eligible for society again." Changes in the 1960s and 1970s forced the order to give up many of their homes, and that changed their focus. Sister Madonna eventually transferred to the Sisters for Christian Community, an order whose members were expected to go out into the world and choose their own work. Since then she has served as a guardian ad litem, assisting in cases where children are involved in the courts. Now officially retired, she volunteers at a jail substation in her community where people report neighborhood problems.

But most of all, Sister Madonna's vocation today is running, as it has been since she discovered it over twenty-five years ago, and competing in triathlons. She was introduced to running at a retreat in 1978 by a Catholic priest who said it harmonizes the body and soul. When she was fifty-two, she competed in the 26.2-mile Boston Marathon, collecting pledges for donations to multiple sclerosis research. Since then she's run nearly forty marathons, in addition to those she has run as part of the more than three hundred triathlons she's participated in, including thirty-four Ironman triathlons. The Ironman is a triathlon on steroids: competitors swim 2.4 miles, ride 112 miles on a bicycle, and then run a marathon. When she was seventy-five, Sister Madonna became the oldest woman to complete the Hawaii—the original—Ironman. She has held age-group records in the Hawaiian and Canadian competitions and participated in twelve world championship triathlons as a member of Team USA. She has a raft of medals and awards, and her accomplishments have garnered her invitations to give motivational speeches.

Sister Madonna is unabashedly and justly proud of these achievements. In her late seventies, she is the picture of fitness: slim, muscular, deeply tanned, looking nowhere near her age. She has the self-possession of the successful athlete: confident, invigorated, and not the least bit out of breath after her weekly forty-mile bicycle excursion. She has strong opinions and expresses them with vigor.

Early on, she received tacit approval from her bishop to run in marathons for charity. After that, Sister Madonna was not deterred by the disapproval of some of her colleagues. She believes she is using God-given talent, and she doesn't apologize. She knows she is fortunate that she can still do what she does, but she also believes—because of the many men and women who tell her so—that she is a pioneer and an inspiration to others. It is a different kind of gratification from what she receives from the women she helped when they were troubled girls. Some come back to see her to let her know they are doing well and to tell her that they still remember what she told them when they were in her care.

Sister Madonna's path is unlike any of the other women, yet they share many qualities. Becoming a nun takes persistence and courage, and so does coming back to competition at seventy after a cycling accident left her with fourteen stitches in her face, a broken scapular, and multiple abrasions and bruises. Her athletic career has been innovative, as was her choice of a new order, which was stimulated by the changes introduced by Pope John Paul II. It wasn't the life her parents intended, but it is fulfilling for her. And it reflects the changes that travelers on the Wisdom Trail have turned to their advantage.

Two

Improvising a Life

Making do with what was available and seizing opportunities as they came were virtues in hard times. Part of the legacy of growing up during the Depression and World War II was an understanding of the value of improvisation. It helped people survive and thrive in years when jobs were scarce and pay was low. They were also patriotic virtues. People on the home front learned to cope with shortages of gasoline and certain foods, and rationing was a fact of daily life. They managed to get along without absent sweethearts or husbands and to live within the limited means of soldiers paychecks. Enterprising girls and young women found a kind of freedom in this climate. It offered room for them to redefine their lives without violating societal constraints.

Then, too, the tasks of the housewife were becoming less all-consuming, and women could find a little unclaimed time. After 1945, as the great wartime manufacturing capacity of this country trained its sights on the civilian market, a myriad of new home conveniences earned the Good Housekeeping Seal of Approval. K-ration technology found its way into convenience foods. American industry saw a marketing bonanza in the homemaker and made the most of it. *Good Housekeeping* and such competitors as the *Ladies Home Journal*, the *Woman's Home Companion*, and *House Beautiful* joined in singing the joys of housewifery, and of managing a family with the help of the shiny new aids.

These factors eased the life of the homemaker and opened up room for expansion. The time-saving goods also stimulated women to work to help pay for them. Many women who went to work during the war did not quit when it was over. Others started work after the war to support husbands who were attending college thanks to the GI Bill, which made college possible but didn't give enough to support a family. So while the woman as homemaker was still queen of the late 1940s through the 1950s, there was an undercurrent; women were looking outward, and entering into activities outside the home. If they were wise or lucky enough to get an education, they were ahead of the game, and ready to step out into the community in some way.

Given the social and commercial attention focused on the lady of the house, working outside the home was frowned on, and day care was almost nonexistent, so women who wanted more from life than homemaking improvised. They said yes to possibilities without knowing what would follow, gravitated toward activities and causes they thought would benefit their community, and sought opportunities they could squeeze in without disrupting their family. They didn't have grand ambitions to save the world, and they were not afraid to jump in at the bottom and work hard. They wanted to use their energy and talents in a wider arena.

These women seldom had a plan. But with a drive to accomplish more than the ordinary, they seized any openings they found. If they were married, they looked for ways to satisfy their desire to use their talents and express their values without neglecting their responsibilities at home. If they were single, they sought ways to support themselves that satisfied their interest in being of service.

"Patricia Radcliffe" says about her career: "I'd like

to be able to tell you it was planned. It wasn't at all. In fact, I didn't expect to have a career, other than marrying and having children, like my mother did. My dad even said, 'Be sure to get a teaching certificate, just in case.'" That pretty well sums up the early lives of most women of this generation. In fact, Patricia did not marry or have children. She did have two careers, and continued long past retirement age sharing the knowledge gained in a lifetime of working for a living.

Patricia took a more direct route to a career than most of the women on the Wisdom Trail. Having been active in student activities at her own university, she accepted an internship in the dean of women's office, to see if she would like that kind of work. One year out of college, serendipity struck: She got a job as assistant dean of students at Beloit College. She stayed for five years and found she loved it.

Her next move was to a larger school, the University of Wisconsin, where she worked on a variety of women's programs, from housing to academic affairs to counseling. Then several deans she knew from other colleges suggested her for a position as dean of women at Swarthmore College. "It was a great college, a great job, another part of the country—and a big challenge," she says.

She continued moving toward more responsibility, more learning, more challenges. After ten years at Swarthmore, though, her luck changed. An opening for vice president of campus life at a university seemed like a step up, but turned out to be a bad move. The post had been empty for a year, and two young assistants had been running the office. She says, "They weren't interested in having another person, let alone a woman, come in and take over. So instead of collaboration and cooperation, they caused me a lot of trouble." Just before the end of the school year, she was fired.

Patricia now sees that as a good thing, but "at the time, it was really the lowest, most painful time of my life so far." She packed up and went home to Michigan for three years. During this period she faced the fact that she was an alcoholic, and entered a recovery program. She also had an appointment as a visiting scholar at the University of Michigan. A friend from there had become dean at a small college. He called her to say he needed help and asked her to join him. Unfortunately, this turned out to be another unhealthy environment. She stuck it out, but she was miserable, physically as well as mentally; she experienced two major health problems—gallbladder surgery and a long bout of pneumonia. She needed to find another job, but the job market was pretty bleak.

Then she got some good advice from the friend she'd gone to join. He said, "Pat, I know why you're not finding a job. You're not looking in the right place. Why don't you do what you're good at? Why don't you hang up your shingle and go into private practice?" She had been trained as a therapist, and had earned a doctorate in counseling psychology, but she hadn't felt confident enough to do it on her own. His belief in her helped her see that she could.

Thus began the second half of her career, built on risk taking, improvising, and persevering. She says, "The process was totally terrifying. Would anyone come to see me? Do I know enough to be a good therapist? But I did it anyway. I had my first client the very first week, and then they just kept coming." After her practice was established, she took another big risk, and started over in a more appealing city. It was her last move, and it brought her fulfillment. Looking back, she says, "One of the high points for me was being successful in private practice, opening my own office and having it work, and being able to help others in their healing. And I did it twice."

Both of her careers gave her a role in helping

others, whether it was young college women or therapy clients. Pat is thoughtful, articulate, a good listener, and someone who gains the trust of others very quickly. Her willingness to share her own most painful moments reveals a commitment to use her life to offer help and demonstrate trust to others.

Shirley Medalie didn't have a plan either, but not long after graduating from college with a degree in psychology, she fell into a job that suited her to a T. Unsatisfied after a few months of volunteering, she went to an employment agency. They sent her to the Statistical Research Group at Columbia University, part of a federal agency set up by President Franklin Roosevelt. It was a secret group that eventually became part of the Manhattan Project; they were developing the atom bomb. She was hired to destroy top-secret documents, but when she said she had learned statistics as a psychology major, she was assigned to more important work.

It was a fascinating place to work, and it was fun. "We had such a good time; we laughed all the time." She and the other girls in the office, mostly young math graduates from well-respected girls' colleges, thought the scientists, who had doctorates from the likes of MIT, were nerds. After the war, the men became famous; two of them won the Nobel Prize.

A year later, the man Shirley had been dating since her sophomore year in college asked her to come to Nevada, where he was stationed by the Navy, and marry him. So she went, to fulfill her goal of being a wife and mother. From then on, she spent her life raising her children and befriending people in all walks of life. Along the way she took up the art of enameling, and that became a lifelong pursuit. Her work was sought after by jewelers, but she chose not to take a commercial route. Instead, she combined her artistic talent with her nurturing nature and volunteered to teach art therapy classes at New York Hospital. It makes her happy to do the two things she likes, helping people and being creative, at the same time. Shirley is attractive and witty, affectionate toward her "adoptees," and has a mischievous smile.

There is no way Emily Korzenik could have even dreamed the way her life would unfold. She married ten days after graduating from Vassar, and her first child was born a year later. Three more would follow. So she found herself with a home in the suburbs and a husband who supported the family. But her education had instilled in her a feeling that she should be doing something worthwhile. Like many of her peers, Emily's first foray into the world beyond her home was as a volunteer. She took the opportunity to raise money for Adlai Stevenson's second presidential campaign, carting campaign signs around the area with her three children, one an infant, in tow. Then she identified a problem with the way the political system worked in her comfortable suburb. It was run by a small group of insiders who were reelected regularly, and few other people bothered to vote. She and a college professor ran for two of the local offices, opposing establishment incumbents. Emily cheerfully admits, "I was just being a gadfly." She and her partner both lost, as they expected. But by offering a choice, they succeeded in getting voters out in significant numbers and creating a more open system.

Emily's next move was a run for the New York State Assembly. She lost that election too, but the effort was worthwhile. She hadn't expected to win, but she was proud that she beat her well-financed primary opponent with fliers printed on a mimeograph machine and a cadre of friends who helped with mailings and telephone calls. In the general election she was able to raise controversial issues because she wasn't afraid of speaking up and she wasn't afraid of losing.

Emily kept improvising as she entered her thirties. While she'd been running for office, she'd also been selected as president of her synagogue. Although

it was a congregation in which women played a sub-
stantial role, she was only the second woman to hold
that position. It was a predictable accomplishment for
her, given the strong grounding in her faith she had
been given by her parents. But she still hadn't settled
on a long-term direction; she hadn't yet found that
"something important" her professors expected of
their women graduates.

When her youngest child entered kindergarten,
though, Emily took a big step away from the bridge-
playing life. She went back to school for a master's
degree in teaching social sciences. When she found
a teaching job, her extrafamilial activities and her
home life met head-on. When she tried teaching
three-quarter time, her teenage daughter told her
firmly, "Mom, you can't do this, because you don't
have enough time for me." So Emily adapted. For
the next five years she taught history part-time, until
the school system elected to end part-time teaching
positions.

As her teaching career was sputtering, the last of
her children was going away to college. Emily learned
that a reform rabbinical college had just ordained its
first woman rabbi, and that appealed to her. Emily
went back to school again and became a rabbi. A
small liberal congregation asked her to serve them

even before she had completed her studies and been ordained. Everything came together: her sense that she should make a difference; her store of affection as a wife and mother; her ability to adapt to whatever a situation demanded; her capacity for empathy; and her talent for seizing opportunity in the service of a cause. For the next twenty-five years that part of her life not devoted to her family was spent in service to her congregation, which thrived under her leadership.

The women of Emily's generation created lives that were gratifying for themselves and for the world around them by starting small, slipping into openings, adjusting to fit everything in, and improvising to expand from there. They were drawn to finding solutions to social problems and making good things happen. The fact that most of them were married and did not have to make a living gave them a platform from which they could survey the landscape and choose their direction without too much concern for what or whether it paid.

One factor that helped shape our women's choices and set them on their ambitious pathways was having role models who paved their way. Several of them had mothers who worked outside the home, and that offered their daughters some notion of career possibilities. Ruth Lubic's first career began when she was fourteen. As early as she can remember, her mother worked in the family pharmacy. Ruth went to work there after her father died, and stayed on for seven years after high school before she decided to become a nurse.

A month before Ruth completed her training, she married Bill Lubic and after graduating moved with him to New York, where she began her nursing career in a cancer hospital. She continued her education by completing a bachelor's degree at Columbia and a master's degree in teaching medical-surgical nursing. The birth of a son, their only child, was the catalyst that helped her find her true calling. She and Bill had been married five years before they were able to conceive a child, and they were very moved by the experience of his birth. Their obstetrician was a pioneer in encouraging fathers to be in the delivery room, and Bill had coached Ruth during the twenty-four hours of her natural, unanaesthetized labor. Ruth was given her baby to breastfeed immediately after he was born, and she and Bill were alone with their new son for the first hour of his life.

The women of the Wisdom Trail, moving on their unplanned, improvisatory tracks, often benefited from luck: a chance encounter, an opening that popped up, a suggestion at the right moment. The alert improviser capitalizes on unexpected events and risks leaping in uncharted but promising directions. Ruth Lubic is a firm believer in serendipity. She was lucky to find an unusual, progressive physician, and she had the wisdom to listen to the advice he gave her. When she told him that her experience giving birth was making her consider going into maternity care, he suggested that she study midwifery.

Ruth had no idea what that was, but when she learned that it was a way to help women have safer, more intimate and caring childbirth experiences, she knew it was what she was meant to do. She enrolled in one of the first programs in the country to train midwives. This avenue eventually led her to establish three birthing centers staffed by nurse-midwives, two of them located, by design, in areas with the highest infant mortality rates in the nation.

When Ruth completed her training, however, she couldn't find a job. At the time, physicians didn't consider midwives qualified to attend births. She went to work as a parent educator for the Maternity Center Association, eventually becoming its director. She began to develop her first birthing center, on Manhattan's Upper East Side. With remarkable perseverance and courage, Ruth led a group that surmounted all the obstacles that members of the medical establishment raised to prevent the center from opening.

Once the clinic was open and successful, she opened another one that would bring safe and comfortable childbirth to the poor. She chose the South Bronx; the area's infant mortality rate was the second highest in the nation, topped only by Washington, D.C. There was opposition from local officials who were resentful of white people coming in and telling mothers how to care for their babies. Adapting her tactics to this situation, she partnered with a local community health center. When her clinic was on a sound footing, she turned it over to the local community. Ruth's experience in the Bronx convinced her that she needed a better understanding of different cultures to do her work, so she earned a doctorate in anthropology. She wrote her dissertation on barriers to innovation in the health care delivery system.

The year after Ruth left the South Bronx clinic, she was awarded a John D. and Catherine T. MacArthur Foundation "genius grant." She chose to use the $375,000 as seed money for another birth center, this time in the heart of one of Washington, D.C.'s most impoverished areas. She had to find and acquire the space, partners, and funding sources, as well as secure permits and approvals before work could begin. Motivated by a powerful desire to solve a pressing social problem, she employed her skills of improvising, adapting, and persevering to bring it off. The success of the center in delivering healthy babies in a warm, homelike setting didn't inoculate it from continuing financial crises, but Ruth keeps fighting for it. The memory of her mother's yellow ring, hocked regularly to buy medicine for the poor, spurs her still.

WORKING FOR A cause they believe in is the great motivator for women of the Wisdom Trail and their chief source of gratification as they look back on their lives. Social problems stimulated their perseverance and bolstered their courage to find imaginative solutions.

Like her fellow trailblazers, Janet Lieberman took some time to find her direction, but when she did she tackled it energetically. As a girl she had found freedom in her family's limited expectations and capitalized on the benign neglect. Although her mother had taught school before she was married, she gave it up when she had children. No one suggested anything to Janet about having a career; that idea came from another source. She vividly remembers the effect on

her when the journalist Helen Gahagan Douglas spoke
to a school assembly when Janet was a junior in her
all-girls high school. This successful, good-looking
woman with a glamorous career as a writer spoke
about the excitement of being a professional, having a
career, and enjoying competition, and it was a revelation for Janet. She thought, Why can't I?

Janet's path was not direct. She married after one
year away at college, finished her bachelor's degree
at nearby Barnard College, and had two sons. For
a few years she led the conventional life of a young
middle-class wife. But with her second son in nursery school, she became bored and sought intellectual
stimulation. She had enjoyed studying psychology at
Barnard, so she decided to get a master's degree.

After she got her degree, Janet went to work for
the New York City Bureau of Child Guidance as a
psychologist, testing public school children for special
education classes. She was then asked to teach at a new
high school for disruptive girls. She learned a great
deal from the other teachers, though it was difficult
work. She found serious shortcomings in the way the
school system dealt with adolescents, but she knew
that she could not make significant changes without
additional credentials. She went back to school for a
doctorate, and specialized in the teaching of reading.

With her responsibilities at home, it took Janet ten years to finish her PhD, and she needed financial aid to keep afloat during the last year. Then she joined the faculty of Hunter College. She had been divorced during this period, and was a single mother for four years before she married again.

Then the chance of a lifetime came along. She was invited to join the staff creating a new community college, LaGuardia, in Queens. Her friends thought it was a step down from the prestige of a professorship at Hunter, but Janet saw it as an opportunity to use her knowledge and experience to solve a serious social problem. The City University of New York, the coordinating agency for all two- and four-year public colleges in New York City, had announced its open admissions policy in 1970. It would offer admission to all New York City high school graduates. Community colleges provided the main avenue to the university for urban minority students. LaGuardia Community College was being designed expressly to educate these students. Its population would be young people whose education had not prepared them for the city's four-year institutions. Because lack of reading skills was a major problem for this group, remediation was a high priority.

Along with her creative colleagues, Janet improvised new methods of teaching these underprepared
students. Her signature accomplishment was the establishment of the first Middle College High School.
Students who were at risk of failing in their regular
schools were introduced to an innovative and rigorous
high school program on the LaGuardia campus, and
had the option of taking college courses along with
their high school requirements. A large proportion of
them succeeded in this challenging and supportive setting and went on to college, confounding all expectations. Middle College became a national model that
has been replicated in more than thirty colleges around
the country, with support from a number of founda-
tions, including the Bill & Melinda Gates Foundation.

Standing up for themselves and for what they
believe in is a hallmark of Wisdom Trail women.
They learned the art of diplomacy as girls, but eventually freed themselves from being typecast. For those
who had strong role models, this solid sense of self
came earlier. As they moved into larger arenas, all the
women of the Wisdom Trail had the confidence to
defend what they thought was right.

Claudia Thomas was blessed with a strong model
in her mother, who was widowed when Claudia was

three and who supported and led her family for the next twenty-two years. Shaped by her mother's convictions, Claudia was launched into the world knowing how to work and how to value herself. In her first negotiation, she convinced her school principal to let her skip seventh grade and go directly into the eighth. When she entered college, her goal was to be a pediatrician. Her mother, however, insisted that she major in home economics, a more practical choice for a young black woman in those days. But Claudia had learned to cook and sew as a girl and saw no reason to spend time studying that at college. When the college counselor asked her who was paying the bill, Claudia admitted it was her mother. So the counselor helped her negotiate a compromise: She would accept her mother's decree for her major, but she would take a minor in chemistry, satisfying some requirements for premed at the same time.

Claudia's first job after college was the result of being a star in the home economics department. An editor of *Ebony* magazine visiting the campus discovered her talent and invited her to go to Chicago and work for the magazine. It was a glamorous job. The most fashionable black women appeared in the pages of *Ebony*, and Claudia saw them all. Glamour only went so far with her, however, and she decided to opt out of a world she found artificial. Her mother had sensed Claudia's dissatisfaction and told her about an opening for a chemistry teacher back in North Carolina. Claudia seized on it and embarked on the teaching career she had never intended. But she found that she loved it, and she's been committed to educating people ever since.

Claudia married an army man and took time out to raise two sons. The army eventually stationed her husband at Fort Lewis, Washington, and they made their home in the nearby town of Lakewood. Claudia was hired as only the second African American in a mostly caucasian school district, but when she was passed over for an administrative job, she exposed her school district's failure to hire women as administrators. Her training and her courage eventually won her the vice principalship for which she was so thoroughly prepared.

Claudia was a creative and flexible teacher and administrator. After she had earned her spurs in the vice principal's position, she applied for a principalship. Her superintendent was wise enough to promote her, and to let her choose the school she wanted to lead. Two schools had openings, and Claudia asked the superintendent which one was the more difficult assignment. He named the one with a reputation as a troubled school; she chose that one. She wanted the chance to show that she could turn a troubled school around, and she succeeded. She engaged students and parents in creating a climate of pride and achievement; she told them they shared the school's problems and had to participate in the solution. Her school became a model. After his first observation visit, the superintendent praised Claudia at the next principals' meeting as an example of effective leadership.

She moved on to become assistant superintendent in another district, and after thirteen successful years there, Claudia retired. The next opportunity she seized was to educate in another sphere. She joined the committee planning an incorporated city in the Lakewood area. Her adaptability and willingness to speak up while welcoming others' views served the process well. When the city of Lakewood was born, she was elected to its first city council. She was the first vice mayor, then became the city's third mayor, the first African American woman mayor in the state. True to her passion for meeting young people's needs, her focus as mayor was on youth programs. "I am still an educator," she says.

Many women of our generation found satisfaction in teaching, even though it might have been only one stage in their career. It was a natural choice, one of

the accepted occupations for women and an extension
of the caring and helping characteristics that were
considered women's particular responsibility. Teaching is a focal point for some of the most pressing social
problems and a great arena for problem solvers. It also
calls for courage and creativity. These are all qualities Lorraine Beitler has in abundance, but teaching
wasn't what she expected to do. She had majored in
chemistry in college, and her first job was as a chemist for a perfume company. She married the month
before she graduated from college and went to work
right afterward. Working by herself in a laboratory
was very unsatisfying, and when she developed a rash
from the chemicals, she used it as an excuse to quit.

Fortunately, she had taken education courses, so
she was able to get a job teaching science at a public
junior high school for girls. The student population
was ethnically mixed and largely disadvantaged, and
the area was infested with gangs. Most of the girls
were Puerto Rican or Irish, and they didn't always
get along with each other. They could be loving and
sharing, but they could also be volatile, and some of
them were very tough. Lorraine thrived on these challenges and rewards; as she recalls, it was "the beginning of a tremendous career. These were children I
could help. They were in such need economically and

socially, and they didn't have the advantage of parents supporting them and knowing about education."

Most of the teachers were disdainful of their students, but Lorraine learned to manage them and won them over. Her homeroom was filled with students no experienced teachers wanted. But her childhood experiences helped her understand how to approach them. She improvised ways to foster their enthusiasm for learning science, and they won prizes in competitions against students from academically elite schools like the Bronx High School of Science.

Lorraine left her job when the first of her three children was born, but after they were in school her sister told her about another challenging teaching job. This time she taught remedial English for college-age students who were studying for health-oriented careers at New York City Technical College. She invented creative and student-centered methods to appeal to students who had had little academic success. She took part in battles with the state government to improve the pay of teachers at the colleges, and she won grants to improve their status.

As Lorraine was improvising ways to stimulate her students' learning and managing a growing family, her husband was building a successful insurance business. Later on, while he was recuperating from surgery, he told Lorraine he needed her help with his company. Her career took a new turn: She became chief operating officer for the firm. She was amazed by her own courage because they put her in charge of computers, with which she had little experience. But she learned what she needed to know, and helped improve the flow of client information. She held that job for ten years.

There were still more turns to come in the life Lorraine improvised. While working with her husband, she also volunteered at the Jewish Museum, and became interested in the Dreyfus trial, the infamous story of injustice and anti-Semitism in late nineteenth-century France. She began collecting materials on Dreyfus, and little by little built an extensive collection of photos, posters, and written material. She was asked to take the exhibit to Israel and to show it at several museums in the United States. Eventually she was invited to bring it to West Point as part of the cadets' education in military justice and ethics. The first visit at West Point was so well received that she has since gone back each year to lecture and lead the thoughtful discussions it invariably engenders. This deeply fulfilling project enables her to continue her mission to share knowledge and to reduce prejudice.

Lorraine tells a story to explain why she has been

so involved in activities that serve the community. "Many years ago, when I was at the beauty parlor, a woman came in and was happily prancing around with this pocketbook, picking it up here and putting it down there. I asked if there was something special about it, and the hairdresser said, 'That's the pocketbook of the year. It's a Gucci and cost twelve hundred dollars and you have to wait on line to get it. That's an acquisition.'" Recognizing the emptiness of that attitude, Lorraine has sought satisfaction in higher goals: promoting justice and tolerance. It is her mission.

SOME OTHER WISDOM TRAIL women took a more circuitous route to the place where their qualities could shine. This was especially true if they lived on their own for some time before marrying. That meant that working was a necessity, and they didn't always have a lot of choices. These women needed an extra measure of adaptability to circumstances and the ability to fit their skills to available opportunities.

As a Japanese American girl growing up in California, Elaine Hayes learned to adapt early. When she was eleven, her father contracted tuberculosis and her mother took over his insurance business. Elaine's mother traveled the farming country outside of Sacramento, calling on Japanese American farmers while a housekeeper took care of Elaine and her siblings. That adjustment was minor for Elaine compared to the major disruption in the lives of all Japanese Americans on the West Coast after the United States went to war with Japan. Elaine was at the end of her first year at Sacramento Junior College when she and her family were sent to the internment camp at Tule Lake. Her ability to adapt and improvise was forged there, as she and her fellow internees built a new life under conditions of extreme hardship.

Elaine got her first job in the camp, developing a YWCA group for the recreation program. Later, she took advantage of a new opportunity that allowed college-age internees to leave and go to college. They could only go to colleges in the Midwest, as the government would not permit them to go back to the West Coast. Elaine left the camp for a small college in Wisconsin and studied there for one year, until her family could no longer afford to pay her way. She needed to support herself, and she had minimal qualifications for doing that. She moved to Chicago to look for work, and found a job at the Curtis Candy Company. It was boring and hot and dirty, but she was allowed to send free boxes of Butterfingers and Baby Ruth bars to her family and friends in the camp.

She also enjoyed meeting people from the different ethnic groups who worked there. Nevertheless, she quit after a month and found work as a file clerk at an insurance company. She worked out so well that her supervisor asked her to find more workers like herself, and eventually she brought ten more Japanese American girls into the office.

At this point, the only cause Elaine was serving was survival. Her next job, in the office of the American Council on Race Relations, introduced her to issues that were important to her, and to people who were intelligent, well educated, and articulate about them. There she met Ralph Hayes, the African American man she would marry.

Ralph was still in college, and when he transferred from Northwestern to the University of Washington he asked her to come to Seattle and marry him. She went on one condition—that she could find work. For the next few years, while Ralph worked nights as a janitor to finish his degree, she had office jobs with the American Friends Service Committee and the University YMCA. She adapted to the prevailing racial climate by applying for jobs with organizations that were the least likely to be biased, but even so she felt she had to tell them that her husband was African American, in case that was a barrier to being hired.

After Ralph finished his degree and could work full time, their first child was born, and Elaine quit working. She still had not had the luxury to think about any cause beyond making a living. Her children led her to her true calling. She began participating in a parent cooperative preschool sponsored by the community colleges in Seattle. Soon she was chairwoman of the coop parents' league in the Central District, where ethnic minorities were concentrated. When her youngest child was about two years old, the college coop faculty asked Elaine to be a part-time instructor. This is the way some women found their direction, though it is more accurate to say that their direction found them. They were in the right place, a job needed to be done, there was an invitation, and they said yes.

In 1966, several years after Elaine became involved in the parent cooperatives, an opportunity came along that her work with them had prepared her for. President Lyndon Johnson's poverty program included funding for day care centers to enable impoverished parents to work and go to school. Because of Elaine's leadership as a parent and instructor in the coop program, the community group that won the local day care grant nominated her to direct the program. Elaine thought it was too big a job to do while raising a family, but she said yes and opened day-care centers throughout the city, improving the lives of countless poor mothers and their children.

Before she set up the first federally-funded centers, there were virtually no day care facilities in the city, and none for children of color. Elaine had the skills to improvise solutions to the problems of developing a huge new program, creating systems that involved stakeholders in program planning, met the budgetary and reporting requirements of the grants, and kept key political supporters informed. She was able to meet the needs of the clients and the mandated goals of the grant. She opened the centers, kept them functioning, and stood up for them against critical constituents and bureaucratic maneuvers to divert funds to other projects. In later years she would be recognized publicly for her achievements.

Elaine personifies the women who had a long, slow start. She is modest, but her accomplishments are remarkable. She has incredible recall of other people's achievements, including those of her accomplished husband, but is reticent about herself. She is a petite woman and a lively and energetic talker.

Elaine's family background and her experience as a Japanese American prepared her to improvise a life worth living. She proves that taking a circuitous route on the Wisdom Trail can be valuable. Detours can turn into advantages for the person who is open to improvisation.

Career counselors advise their clients that multiple skills and experiences are useful in the job market, but that wasn't clear to women who found their way without guidance. The entry-level jobs women held before their babies came and the volunteer work at their children's schools didn't seem to be rungs on a career ladder. Entrepreneurial and persistent women, however, discovered that every experience counts.

When Julie Hungar applied for the job that would launch her career, she was forty-one years old, a wife, and a mother of four children. Before her housewife years, Julie had worked at radio and television stations, earned a bachelor's degree, and started on a master's degree. She didn't complete that degree until after her second child was born, when her forward-looking husband urged her to go back and finish it as insurance in case she ever needed to support herself, though they agreed that she should stay home with their children. To keep active, she took on leadership responsibilities in several arts organizations and volunteered in her children's schools, tutoring and instigating a movement to address segregation in the schools.

As her children grew older, being a volunteer was no longer enough to satisfy her. She wanted the responsibility and recognition that comes with a real job—with a salary. She set her sights on teaching at Seattle Central Community College, which appealed to her because of the college's diverse student body. Despite having only one year of college teaching experience, her persistence won her a part-time position, but when she applied for a full-time opening, she expected competition. She was lucky, though. The position was teaching English in college vocational programs, and applicants had to have three years' experience in the working world. Julie's years of working to pay for college as a radio and TV writer counted. None of the other in-house part-timers had her qualifications. The last hurdle was an interview with the famously autocratic dean of instruction. When he asked her why she was right for the job, she blurted, "Because I've raised four children." She got the job and loved it. The students were older than the typical college student, and many had not done well in high school and were eager for a second chance. She felt she was doing something that mattered.

The jobs she'd held to earn her way to college, volunteering and observing in her children's classrooms, even being a parent contributed to her ability to improvise, adapt, and persist in getting that first job.

Other equally improvisational women found satisfactory careers working as volunteers. That path also required persistence and adaptation, and, since there was no financial reward, it was a labor of love. Their reward was in solving problems and enriching other people's lives.

Like many of her peers, Selma Fink taught school before she was married. Her husband was eleven years older than she and since he had a well-established medical practice, she quit teaching when she became pregnant with their first child and never went back. Selma rented a studio for sculpting; she had always loved using her hands and had taken a sculpture course when she was single. It was an ideal pursuit for a mother, and the beginning of a lifelong career. Creating something tangible out of her own spirit and ideas gave her endless satisfaction.

Selma also enjoyed working in a sculpture center with others in her neighborhood. Once her children were in school, she and an artist friend offered to teach a class at a center for the blind. After five years the project was taken over by the center's staff, so she began teaching in her own basement studio. With her

sense of appreciation for beauty and her positive outlook, she has shared her art and given others in her
community the opportunity to express the creativity
that she has enjoyed.

Selma has a warm personality and the trace of a
Southern accent, which adds to her charm. Her simple
manner belies the depth of her intelligence. Although
she has known suffering, her spirit of adventure has
not dimmed. She is empathic and has a gift for friend-
ship. These traits make her an ideal source of inspiration for aspiring artists.

Nell Berry has enjoyed a rich life serving her community in organized and informal settings. Her talent
for helping others was evident when her two children
held a party for her eightieth birthday. At least 110 guests
showed up from all across the country. Family, neighbors, and other air force wives whom she had befriended
when they were young and learning their roles were
among the people who traveled to help her celebrate.

Nell had worked at an ordnance plant during
World War II after attending college. She married in
1944. After that, there was no question of a career, as
her husband's work took them all over the country.
The first time her daughter was in the same school
for more than one year was in high school. Nell was
an at-home mom, who helped her daughter and son

adjust to all their moves and supported her husband as a dutiful officer's wife. Along the way, she did volunteer work at the bases where he was stationed, helping younger wives and their families adapt to the service.

After her husband was killed on a test flight, Nell moved to a new home near an air force base outside San Antonio and began to build a settled life. Having been alone during much of her marriage, she knew she could manage on her own. Her husband's pension gave her enough to live on, so she was able to keep volunteering with organizations such as Meals on Wheels. Nell stayed active with the air force wives' groups, continuing to help orient new Air Force families and keeping in touch with a far-flung network of friends from the service. She looks for people in her community who need her help and is ideally suited to the role she has created for herself. Comfortable to talk with, friendly and unassuming, she's easy to trust. She likes to have a good time, too; she still plays golf and, she says, "I go dancing if I have someone to dance with." She is close to the members of her large and loving family. As the sixth of nine children, she is a nurturing Aunt Nell to twenty-three nieces and nephews.

There are downsides to volunteering, though, and Ruth Feder knows the rewards and the difficulties.

On balance she has found satisfaction and real pleasure in what she accomplished as a volunteer.

Ruth grew up in a close-knit family that lived in a two-family house with her mother's immigrant parents. Ruth liked school and excelled there; she was deeply involved with and influenced by her teachers. Education was emphasized in her family, and her parents gave her a great deal of freedom. She spent most Saturdays at the Brooklyn Historical Society or the children's museum. When her public high school entered her science project in a competition at the American Museum of Natural History in Manhattan, she slept in the museum to be on time for the competition.

Although Ruth's mother did not have a career, she had started a nursery school during World War II to take care of children whose mothers worked while the fathers were away at war. When Ruth was thirteen and fourteen she helped with the women's group her mother had organized during the war; they rolled bandages for wounded soldiers, making it easier for doctors to speed their care. Ruth married right after graduating from college, just before her nineteenth birthday, and went to work. Her first job was with a publishing company; she was an editorial assistant in the mathematics textbook department.

Following her mother's advice to get an education degree, Ruth went to graduate school at night and earned her teaching certificate. Then she spent two interesting and challenging years teaching second graders. Her first school was on a street in the heart of the drug world and many of her pupils did not speak English at home. Parents only risked sending their children to school through those dangerous streets because they received free breakfasts and lunches. Ruth was shocked by the hunger and found the circumstances heartbreaking; she learned a great deal and was fond of her pupils. "The idea of what I could do to affect other people's lives emerged from that experience."

When her principal moved to another school the following year, she asked Ruth to move with her. The new school was on the West Side of Manhattan, and Ruth's class consisted of top-achieving, upper-middle-class white students. Halfway through the year, a group of Puerto Rican immigrants were added to the class. Many of them were just learning English. She was able to use the skills she acquired at her first school to meet the needs of two very different sets of students.

Ruth's career as a teacher ended when her husband accepted a research position at Harvard Law School, and they moved to Cambridge, Massachusetts. Her teaching experience enabled her to get another job in publishing, this time editing training textbooks for reading teachers. She loved the job, but after two years in Cambridge, they moved back to New York. Their first child, a daughter, was born soon after they returned, and while she was an infant, Ruth had the opportunity to write a remedial math booklet for the New York City schools. It was the last time she worked for pay. After that she began volunteering, and she has employed her considerable energy and organizational talent ever since as a volunteer for a number of prominent organizations involved with libraries and the arts.

She began immediately to look around for something worthwhile to do. She found a community leadership course offered by the Citizens' Committee for Children of New York, where she learned about civic activities in health, education, juvenile justice, welfare, and state politics. She knew how lucky she was—she didn't need to earn a living, and had time to work at something that would make a contribution.

Ruth took leadership responsibilities in a number of these organizations, and she still serves them. Her volunteer work has been thoroughly engrossing and her accomplishments are deeply satisfying. One of the lessons she learned growing up was that she could do anything she wanted to do if she put her mind to it, and that she shouldn't be restricted by people who told her she couldn't. She was bright and energetic and wanted more responsibility and challenge than she found as a schoolteacher. It's clear from all she achieved that she could have had a successful professional career if she had chosen to. But when she began to achieve success she realized that her work was affecting her home life; she also did not want to compete with her husband. She made a conscious decision not to pursue a career.

Ruth does not doubt that she made the right decision. Her marriage has been fabulous and she is proud of her husband's success. She says, though, "It would have been nice to have a career. One of the troubles with the life I've lived in volunteering is that there's no ladder of success like there would be in a career."

One of her most rewarding activities is with the MacDowell Colony, the oldest artists' colony in the United States. She has served on its board for a number of years, and has given time, energy, and thought to improving it and bringing it to the public's attention. Nurturing artists and enabling them to try something new is a way, she says, to affect the whole cultural life of the United States. Another organization with which she has been heavily involved is the Smithsonian's Archives of American Art, "the world's largest and most widely used resource dedicated to collecting, preserving, and making available for study the papers and primary records of the visual arts in America." The papers are used by art dealers and curators planning exhibits. Ruth says, "Collecting the history of art in America was the importance of the archives for me."

Support for the arts is a consistent theme in her activities, and she has used her energy, intelligence, and organizing and fund-raising skills to make a difference in these organizations and for the people and institutions they benefit. "I would be a very unhappy camper if I didn't have the work I do, and the sense of being able to affect my world.

"I really like what I do," Ruth says. "I like the fact that I have variety, yet my work all comes together and interacts." Volunteering has given her the satisfaction of personal growth as well. "I feel very lucky because, whether it's warranted or not, I have a sense of strength and ability to think through a problem. It forms who I am as a person."

Ruth is thoughtful and direct. She "tells it like it is," but with wisdom, honesty, and judgment. She is modest, but it's clear that she is intelligent, well organized, and giving. She puts all her skill and talent into the service of the organizations she supports.

For the women who never married, having a career was not a matter of choice. They might have been interested in improving the lives around them, but they had to do that while making a living. These women were drawn to careers in which they could make a difference. They share the Wisdom Trail quality of service to the community, and they show that there are many routes to the well-lived life.

Jean Phillips followed a path of her own making, free of family expectations, like Janet Lieberman. Unlike Janet, Jean never married. Jean characterizes her path as "zigzagging." She is the model of improvisation, of traveling without an itinerary. She followed byroads and took loops until she found the place she belonged. Her parents were divorced and her mother lived alone, then her father died, so home was her grandparents' house in Massachusetts. As a young adult, she developed a pattern of going off to take an easy job and then coming back home for a while. She was an adult babysitter; she taught swimming at the town pool and at a summer camp; she went to college and earned a bachelor's degree; she served as camp counselor for a couple of years; she earned a master's degree in history; and she did housekeeping at a ski lodge.

Then she took a giant step and joined the Air Force. She was commissioned a second lieutenant and succeeded so well in that position that she almost signed up again at the end of her four-year tour of duty. She thought better of it, though, and went back home and resumed her old routine. Back at work at the summer camp, she had the lucky encounter that would lead to her life's work. One day the doctor at the camp said to her, "There's something you do, and there's a school for it. You help people."

The doctor told her about two universities that had opened master's degree programs for college student service professionals, and she suggested that Jean would be good at it. Jean made one more detour, a short stint as a personnel counselor at Jordan Marsh, Boston's big department store, then she applied and was accepted in the student services program at Syracuse University. Two years later she had her master's degree. She applied for a job opening at Carleton College.

Jean found her place there. She stayed at Carleton until retirement. She had one more play to make, though, and that was to take a stand for herself in the men's world of academic administration. She had been promoted within the women's program, eventually becoming dean of women. In 1970, after she had served five years in that role, the college president decided to reorganize and have one dean of students manage the men's and women's programs. He told Jean, "I respect what you do, and I would like to consider you for the position, but it's not a job for a woman." She answered, "It's not whether it's a job for a woman, it's whether I'm the woman for the job." Startled by her own firmness, she nevertheless recognized it was long overdue—and she got the job.

Jean now recognizes what propelled her back to the safety of jobs for which she was overqualified: a reluctance to be in charge or to be in front of people. This moment changed all that and freed her. In both positions, she helped lead the college through the difficult but exhilarating sixties and seventies, when the rules were changing in areas such as student housing. Speaking up for herself gave her the confidence to be an effective dean for all students while supporting women's efforts to break down the barriers that had held them back. She collaborated with students, faculty, and other staff to make Carleton truly coeducational, and to reduce the feeling of separate men's and women's colleges sharing the same campus.

The years of zigzagging and her time in the air

force gave Jean a broad base of experience with different kinds of people that served her well in her college career. She is flexible, tolerant of diverse viewpoints, even-tempered, and goal-oriented. However difficult the problem, she finds a solution and maintains the respect of those who may have disagreed with her. Her great satisfaction was in her role as counselor, the role revealed to her by the camp doctor.

The women of the Wisdom Trail improvised their pattern of progress, whether they took up volunteering, or went back to school, or said yes to a job offer, or took a wise adviser's suggestion to heart. They risked disapproval, discouragement, ridicule, and failure as they pushed the limits of the narrow role set in their early years. They enthusiastically stretched the boundaries that limited their lives. Without knowing what lay ahead, they saw uncertainty as opportunity and made the most of it.

THREE

Living with or without Men

When the girls who were Jazz Age and Depression-era babies were growing up, the issue of men's and women's roles was not a common topic of conversation. We had our heroines, and Eleanor Roosevelt was one of them. But she came with the rarified air of old wealth and the tremendous political power of her husband. Though we admired her, no one expected to achieve her status. Amelia Earhart was another. Her achievements were spectacular precisely because she was a woman performing in a man's world. She expected that her exploits in the air would signal a significant breakthrough for women, and her view of marriage was consistent with her independent and self-determinate stance. She described her marriage to George Putnam as "a partnership with dual control," and insisted on keeping her own last name. She inspired the barn-storming women pilots who starred in the air shows of the 1930s, but beyond that she was an anomaly. The glamorous vision of the independent woman flew right into the headwinds of the Depression and crashed.

For ordinary folks, family life was the norm: Men were the breadwinners; women managed at home. But these roles were complicated by the Depression. Deepening poverty strained marriages as men lost their jobs and women had to scrimp to keep their families fed. Defeated men hoping to find work sometimes abandoned their families; others uprooted them to hunt for jobs in less stricken areas of the country. Wives contributed to the family finances, but they did it at home—taking in boarders, sewing, selling eggs or baked goods. None of these things had any noticeable effect on the general relations between men and women. The economic order was turned upside down, and poverty interfered with the normal workings of the family, but the accepted family constellation did not change appreciably. It was the way things were, and people didn't talk about it.

In fact, there were a lot of things people didn't talk about. Engaged couples didn't ordinarily discuss whether they would have children, never mind planning how many they would have. They assumed they would live near wherever the husband worked and that their children would go to school in their neighborhood. They would have one car. And the wife would be a homebody.

There were two main routes to the life of happily ever after: Girls either got married right out of high school, or they found a husband before they left college. Anyone who missed those chances found a job to support herself until Mr. Right came along to take over. Girls thought about the kind of man they would marry, but there was a measure of happenstance in the actual choosing. The decision to marry was based in part on whatever man was in the picture when the urge to pair up was felt. The men these women chose—or were chosen by—had matching expectations. They would marry, father children, and have a career so they could support their family. High school and college were the best sites for social networking; once out of that network, it was difficult to make connections. In that case, the woman who had the foresight or fortune to land a job where there were plenty of men had the best chance of finding a

husband later. If a woman stayed single, it wasn't nec-
essarily by design. Most of our Wisdom Trail women
expected to marry, but for one reason or another it
just never happened for some of them.

Most of them married soon after graduating from
college and began having babies. Sooner or later, they
started to stir out of the box and look for a little more
stimulation. Housekeeping and childrearing didn't
take up all their energy and didn't give much play to
their interest in the world beyond home. They knew
they would have to fulfill their desires for a richer life
in ways that meshed with their marriage.

During the five years of World War II, roles became
blurred. Women could not only take jobs replacing
men who were drafted; for the first time they could
volunteer for military service. Although most of them
served as nurses or clerks, some worked alongside men
as mechanics. But everyone saw the war years as an
interruption in normal life, and people were eager to
get back to normal.

They followed three main routes that were compatible with sustaining home life. The easiest one
was to marry a man who at least accepted, and at best
actively supported, his wife's involvement in activities
outside the house. Barring that, it took skillful adapting and plenty of compromising to keep a husband

feeling comfortable and not challenged by his wife's independence. The third and most difficult path was to persevere in the face of a husband's displeasure and count on the strength of the union to bring him around.

Regardless of the route they took, these women valued their marriages. Caring for husbands and children was a satisfying outlet for their capacity to build and maintain loving relationships. A stable marriage was highly admired; divorce had not yet become the solution of choice for marital problems. They set out to manage double lives within acceptable limits of disruption and for the most part succeeded. They pushed the limits, though, and in doing so helped teach their husbands the advantages of wives who accomplished things on their own.

The early challenges of women on the Wisdom Trail were the same ones faced by today's women: juggling home, family, and an outside life. Finding enough hours in the day for housework, cooking, shopping, and laundry was a challenge then as now. But in the 1950s and 1960s, it was faced solely by the woman, except for the few rare men who shared household and parenting chores. In general, men's attitudes reflected a complicated set of factors, some of which were not easy to talk about. Even if the meals were ready, the beds made, and the laundry done, husbands might not be happy about their wives' activities or might resent their involvement outside the home. Some men also felt threatened by their wives' public success, or were embarrassed by the causes the women supported.

Women who stayed single faced different challenges. Free of the burden of having to satisfy husbands and children, they had, on the other hand, the burden of earning a living. Beyond that, they were on their own to improvise substitutes for the circle of affection that married women enjoyed. Our single women creatively attained that end. They chose careers with a strong social component and developed strong bonds with other women, maintaining satisfying relationships they continue to enjoy in retirement.

Among our women who married, four found just the right man: Ruth Lubic, Charlotte Ward, Alice Dieter, and Elaine Hayes. They had the wisdom to forge relationships that were equal and based on mutual love and respect. Their accomplishments were their own, but their husbands' strong support contributed to their success.

Ruth met the man she would marry on a blind date on New Year's Eve 1952, while she was training to be a nurse; she and Bill were married in May 1955,

and she finished her training that June. They settled in
New York, where Bill practiced law. His parents were
hardworking Croatian immigrants who placed great
importance on education, and he had gotten a liberal
arts degree at Columbia before going to law school.
When Ruth saw how much he had gained from his
education, she regretted not having gone to college.
With his support, she went at night while working
full-time. Then she got a traineeship from Columbia
Teachers College and finished her bachelor's degree
there.

Bill always supported Ruth's work. He managed his own law firm, and spent a lot of time in his
office, including weekends. He understood that Ruth
needed to do the same. She says, "Change is not made
on a forty-hour week. You work incessantly." They
had some help from "a grandmotherly-type person,"
but otherwise they shared everything. They took
turns taking care of their son and doing the housekeeping. "We still do our own housework. Yesterday
I was ironing and he was vacuuming the bedroom.
To me that's what marriage is all about. The initial
rush of love, of physical love and all that, tapers down,
and the most important thing is that we've never been
happier than when we're working together."

Bill still works part-time at his law firm, but he is

fully involved in Ruth's work at the birth clinic. He is on the board and provides free legal work, and he goes with Ruth to all her conferences. He believes so strongly in the importance of the clinic that he cheerfully adjusts his schedule to accommodate hers. Ruth says, "He's not somebody who has to be in the limelight, so he's very supportive of me. He's my best public relations person."

Equal partnerships require partners with self-confidence and the willingness to compromise. Bill Lubic understood that he was marrying a capable, independent woman, so he was prepared to be a more equal partner than the typical man of his generation. Ruth's confidence in their partnership was an asset in confronting obstacles to her goals. She counted him as her first and most important convert.

It worked well for Ruth to marry a man who had a busy life and could relate to her need to pursue her own interests. Charlotte Ward went one step further—she married a fellow scientist. Charlotte knew by the eighth grade that she would be a college professor. She considered herself smart and plain, so she expected to be the stereotypical old-maid schoolteacher. At sixteen, she enrolled in the University of Kentucky, and when she found to her surprise that chemistry was her best subject, it became her major.

She first met Curt Ward, a new graduate student, in her senior physical chemistry class. They were only acquaintances throughout that year, and after graduation she left Kentucky to take a graduate teaching fellowship in chemistry at Purdue University. A year later, Curt finished his master's degree at Kentucky and came to Purdue on a research fellowship. They reconnected in a chance meeting in the student union building. Charlotte invited him to dinner as a potential date for her roommate, but she wound up marrying him herself at the end of that summer.

They agreed they wouldn't have a child the first year they were married. Charlotte, who has a down-to-earth sense of humor, say with a laugh that they just made it. Their daughter Emma was born two weeks late—two weeks after they celebrated their first wedding anniversary. While Charlotte taught her classes and worked toward her degree, Curt stayed home during the day and took care of Emma. They ate supper together, then he worked all night at the lab. When Curt finished his PhD he took a job as an industrial chemist in Tonawanda, New York, and Charlotte and Emma stayed at Purdue so she could finish her course work and research. With that done, they joined Curt in Tonawanda. The plan was for her to write her dissertation, then meet with her adviser when he came to Tonawanda, where he had a consulting contract.

Her adviser, though, saw no reason why a woman with a husband and child needed a PhD, and for over a year he threw obstacles in her path. Then the Wards learned that he was leaving the country for a year. They decided Charlotte would leave the girls with Curt (by now there was a second daughter), go to Purdue, and camp on the adviser's doorstep until he approved her work before he left. Still putting up roadblocks, he added an enormous set of calculations to her requirements, but Charlotte refused to be defeated. She got the work done and was ready for her oral exam. By this time she was very pregnant with their third child. She wore voluminous maternity clothes when she went to defend her dissertation, and she remembers thinking that if the all-male committee gave her any trouble, she was prepared to wince at regular intervals, to make sure they let her go in a hurry. That wasn't necessary. She received her diploma by mail when Mark was a week old.

During her first pregnancy, Charlotte had been sick constantly and had daily threatened to drop out of school. Every day, Curt pushed her to go back. Much later, she asked him why. He told her, "I knew you wouldn't be fit to live with if I didn't." She says,

"He supported me in everything." After he joined the faculty of Auburn University in Alabama, Charlotte was invited to teach elementary school science on a television program that was broadcast across the state, and that later led to a teaching career at Auburn. Their family eventually included four children, and Charlotte says Curt was the real nurturer. He liked to cook breakfast, and until he died, he loved to go grocery shopping every day. She says it was a wonderful marriage: "It just didn't last long enough—only forty-seven years."

Alice Dieter found her route to a compatible marriage through shared enthusiasms. She and her husband pursued different careers, but they collaborated to promote causes they both cared about deeply. Les was an engineer who spent much of his working life with the telephone company. Alice had a successful career in journalism, triggered by her epiphany over Hints from Heloise and abetted by her mother, who lived with the Dieters while their children were young. She used her newspaper columns as a forum for issues she believed were significant and not only covered them as a journalist but also acted on her convictions. For instance, she wrote about her belief in civil rights, and Les joined her in lobbying the Idaho legislature to pass the state's first public accommodations law. It banned discrimination on the basis of race, color, religion, or national origin by privately owned facilities such as restaurants, hotels, and theaters that were open to the public.

The couple helped to organize the Boise Valley World Affairs Association to develop international awareness in their community, at a time when local attitudes were insular and isolationist. They often hosted overseas visitors in their home, and these contacts provided grist for Alice's column. They were involved in the city's arts council, and Alice called attention to deserving local arts productions in her column. When Les became interested in quantum mechanics' alternate way of viewing the universe, Alice, a devout Episcopalian, saw theological implications in the subject. Together they gave a lecture and discussion on the concept at church camp, and out of that developed a discussion group that has continued for over twenty years.

They also shared a love of skiing and the outdoors. Alice eventually took a job writing for the public relations department of Boise Cascade, a large national lumber company. After Les took up photography as a hobby, the two of them filed a number of stories about mountain excursions in the region, with her writing and his photos. They also share a love of reading and have always done a lot of it together. Since Les has become legally blind, Alice reads aloud to him, or they listen to audio books.

Her marriage, she says, has been an active delight, and sex has been an important part of it: "Still is, I might add. I don't think people should ever give up on that, though maybe it's at a different level." Alice believes they complement each other. He is quieter and more thoughtful than she; he stabilizes her and she enlivens him. Once, when she had to research a story for Boise Cascade's magazine, she tried to get Les to say that he didn't mind her leaving. He finally said, "If you're feeling guilty about traveling, and you're trying to get me to tell you it doesn't matter so you won't feel guilty, you're not going to get that. Of course I don't like it when you're gone, but that's your job. So you deal with your guilt. It's not my problem." There was no pretense with him, but "he was always a cheerleader if not a participant" in whatever she chose to do.

Elaine Hayes also had her husband's full support. Elaine continued to work after their marriage while Ralph finished college, and she kept working until just before her first child was born. They worked at different institutional levels, but Elaine and Ralph followed careers dedicated to serving the children of the inner city. She provided poor working mothers a safe environment for their children in her day care centers; Ralph was a role model for African American students as a high school teacher in inner-city schools and later in the suburbs. It was not surprising that Ralph always encouraged Elaine's work, including the volunteering she did while she was an at-home mother.

Ralph did have trouble getting used to Elaine's parenting style. She emphasized explanation, a technique influenced by the Japanese approach to child rearing, in which spanking wasn't practiced and family pride and reputation were the main disciplinary factors. Ralph was used to a stricter kind of discipline, but he came to accept her way. It was an example of the accommodations they made to each other's culture. Elaine says they grew to understand each other so well that they often finished each other's sentences.

These women were exceptions for their generation. Having a husband *and* children *and* a career was definitely not the usual thing for married women in the early postwar years. It was a choice: If a woman wanted a career, she usually chose to stay single; if she married, she would try to avoid getting pregnant. Musicians, authors, and dancers were the kinds of people who would stay single, or at least childless, in favor of their careers. Women who married usually did so with the understanding that marriage was their career. Ruth Lubic and Charlotte Ward didn't accept those limitations. Alice Dieter found a career she could develop at home while her children were small, one that was eased by her mother's assistance when she eventually went to work outside her home. They managed to have it all, in the days before that was a concept.

Even when men were supportive of their active wives, accommodating dual careers required flexibility. With husbands who held more traditional views of marriage, wives looking to open their lives to broader interests had to develop a deeper level of adaptability. Wise women who wanted to preserve their marriages as they explored opportunities outside the home were careful not to erode their husbands' confidence in their role as head of the family. This was especially important when a couple shared similar interests and were involved in the same activities.

In this situation, June Chen found a nice balance. Her technique was to start organizations and keep them moving forward, but to let her husband be out in front. She is an energetic and outgoing Taiwanese American, full of ideas and keenly interested in a variety of causes. Both her parents were teachers, and they encouraged her to get an education. After receiving a bachelor's degree in economics from National Taiwan University, she married her college tutor and they moved to Singapore. They were both teachers there, he in college and she in high school. They traveled to the United States for graduate study. June was offered a scholarship at the University of Kansas, but her husband was accepted at the University of Oregon, so they went there. Then they moved to Berkeley, where her husband did additional graduate work. She alternated between studying mathematics and working in an insurance company to support the two of them while he finished his degree. She says, cheerfully, "I got a PHT, Push Husband Through." Then he was hired by Boeing, and they moved to Seattle.

June soon went to work for Boeing too, working her way from an entry-level job to a systems analyst. She worked for ten years, until her second child was born. Then she stayed home to raise her boys, but when they were both in school, she grew bored and frustrated. She was active in the PTA, but she wanted more stimulation, so she joined her local Democratic Party caucus; then she ran for precinct committeewoman. "It was an easy win," she laughs. "I was the only Democrat on the Eastside." She campaigned for local political candidates, Asian and Caucasian, and was one of two Asians and only a few women in the Washington delegation to the 1992 Democratic National Convention. She participated in a trade delegation to China for the Greater Seattle Chamber of Commerce. When a more democratic government came into power in Taiwan, she accompanied Washington Governor Gary Locke, the nation's first Asian American governor, on an official visit there.

June has cheerfully let her husband be the leader in Taiwan American affairs, but that has not cramped her style or limited her involvement. "For ninety percent of the Taiwanese organizations here, I was the founding mother. But I didn't want to be an officer, so my husband was president of the Taiwanese Association and the Taiwan Chamber of Commerce. I started these things in my basement, but I supported him all the way."

The only time she stepped out in front in Taiwanese affairs was to form a local chapter of the Formosan Association for Public Affairs (FAPA). It lobbied on an issue that was controversial with the community, and no one else wanted to lead it. The Chens supported a pro-democracy party that was opposed to the ruling autocracy in Taiwan. Some American Taiwanese feared that if they supported the pro-democracy group, their families in Taiwan might be penalized. When the leader of this faction came to Seattle, the Chens were the only ones who invited him to their home. Their friends came to meet him, and he urged them to form a local FAPA and suggested that June be the president. He also challenged her to educate the younger generation to become involved in politics. That inspired her to help start a summer training program for young Asian Americans.

The basis for June's success in her community and in marriage might just possibly be captured when she says she does what she likes. She told her husband, "When you were teaching, I was teaching. When you were a student, I was a student. When you were working, I was working. When I quit Boeing, I wanted to do whatever I like." And, she adds, "he lets me do it, and I appreciate that." Her method stood the test of time: She is still busy in her community projects, and the Chens celebrated fifty years of marriage in 2008.

It's fun to be around her. She laughs a lot, and is full of lively and surprising stories. Often the joke is at her expense, but she's confident enough to be able to poke fun at herself. June is extremely generous with her wide circle of friends; once introduced into her circle, you are there for life. She's full of ideas for ways to help people, and she energetically enlists her friends in her enthusiasms. She has a serious commitment to democracy and to extending its benefits throughout her community.

The concept of "letting me do what I like" sounds strange in this postliberation age. June is a force of nature whose husband had the wisdom to see that she was going to do what she liked in any case, but giving one's partner a sense that he was consulted was a tool in the adaptation repertoire of women who grew up in preliberation days. They didn't look at it as an infringement on their ability to do what they wanted. They recognized that it might be hard for their men to adjust, and they worked around that obstacle in their own ways.

Joyce Millington's technique came naturally to her. She was treated like a princess by her father when she was growing up in Trinidad. He was a successful accountant, and he was able to make sure that she had a piano, took music lessons, and attended one of the best private high schools in San Fernando, Trinidad's second-largest city. When she graduated she went to work to support herself, first as a telephone operator, and then as a cashier and bookkeeper. At twenty-seven, she married a man thirteen years older. He treated her like a princess too. She learned to manage that relationship in a way that gave her freedom to pursue her own activities.

Since her husband had a comfortable job, Joyce had domestic help, so she quit working when she became pregnant. Then she began to do her "social work." When she was young she didn't understand why her mother was always doing things for people, but after Joyce was married she began doing the same thing. She was president of the local Girl Guides organization and active in an ecumenical group called Church Women United, which organized a project to provide soup for poor children who had no lunch at school. The program spread throughout Trinidad. When workers in the city went on strike, Joyce took food to the strikers. Instead of buying birthday presents for her children, she took them with her to buy school supplies and deliver them to the children of the poor.

Joyce's charity work involved a certain amount of subterfuge to get around her husband's concerns about the cost. Young women today might not be willing to use her method, but she is unapologetic; she knew she was doing good work and she knew they could afford it. She would tell "little lies" when she needed money for one of the families she helped, and she would have a plausible excuse ready if he asked her about it. But he never refused or criticized her. In fact, sometimes when he caught her hiding a package in the grocery basket to take to a family she was helping, he would tease her about her "charity bag."

Although Joyce's later life turned out to be far different from the one she lived in Trinidad, she never lost her zest for life and for lending a hand to others. She has a sense of humor that makes her vibrant and charming. She gives an impression of strength and stability, despite a life of ups and downs. She is open about her story, and comfortable sharing the wisdom she has acquired.

Shirley Medalie has always been a rebel, as her marriage contract makes clear. In 1944 that phrase wasn't part of the courtship lexicon, but Shirley was more independent than most young women her age. "We had a prenuptial. When he proposed, he said, 'I can't wear a ring on my left hand, it's my tennis hand.' I said, 'That's all right, nobody in our family wears rings.' And he said, 'I don't like to play tennis with girls.' I was playing tennis then, but I said, 'All right, then, you don't play with any other girls.' He agreed. Then I said, 'And another thing, I don't like to get up to make breakfast in the morning, so I won't get up for breakfast.' We've stuck to this over the years." It's worked well, too; they have enjoyed more than sixty years together.

. . .

WHAT OF THE WOMEN whose relationship with
their husbands was neither collaborative nor malleable? Boys who came to manhood in the 1940s had
been raised with certain expectations. They were to
be the heads of their households, earn a living, take the
lead in making decisions, be in charge of their family.
They expected their wives to manage the home and
the children, and to be available to them otherwise.
It could be annoying to have a wife spending a lot of
time on volunteer work or making news as an activist
or, most threatening for some men, earning her own
money. In those circumstances a woman had to take
a stand and have confidence that she could show her
husband that his reservations were groundless. She
needed courage to take the risk and the perseverance
to keep going.

Emily Korzenik married ten days after she finished college. Her husband was twenty years older;
she was attracted to him because he was very smart
and intellectually he took her seriously. But when she
decided to get involved in local politics and upset the
entrenched establishment, her husband didn't like the
notoriety. It was stressful for their marriage. This was
at a time when more women were beginning to run

for office, and one day he showed her a newspaper column by a man whose wife was a candidate. The man described how tough it was on him because no matter what he was doing, what his wife did that day was more interesting and exciting. Emily's husband said, "This is where I am."

After ending her forays in politics, Emily thought her next move would be fine with her husband. She wanted to have a job, and once her youngest child was in kindergarten, she decided to go back to school. She chose to work for a master's degree in social sciences so she could either teach school or go on for a doctorate. Her husband didn't object, but he was not supportive. She said to him, "I can't believe it. I married an intellectual man, and he isn't thrilled that I'm taking a master's and would like to be able to teach. I would think you would be pleased about that." She understood that it was hard for him. The only time she could do her homework was at night after the children were in bed. That meant she came to bed very late, and he was not happy about that. But she kept on, and eventually he accepted what she was doing. He gave her the idea for her master's thesis and critiqued it as she wrote it.

After earning her master's degree, Emily taught high school for several years, working only part-time because she wanted to have time for her family. Her final career step was to become a rabbi. When she told her husband she wanted to go to rabbinical school, she says, "There was silence. He was a traditional man. But he let it all happen, and he was very proud of me." Before she was ordained, Emily was selected to be the rabbi for a small congregation. She served there for twenty-five years, retiring at seventy-four after seeing the congregation grow under her leadership. She retired when her husband's health failed and she needed to be available for him. But even in retirement Emily remains active in her community.

Marriages did not always survive among the Wisdom Trail generation, although divorce was much less common than it is today. The usual story had the husband falling for another woman, and yes, she was often younger. There were many different versions among our women, but the significant part is the way they dealt with it and managed to hold things together and make a life for themselves and their children. Today Jeanne Ehrlichman Bluechel is happily married to Allan Bluechel, a former Washington state senator. She has an influential role as a volunteer—she provides music education for public school children—and an active family and social life. Some thirty-five years ago, though, Jeanne took to her bed and didn't

want to get up. Her first husband was John Ehrlichman, who was President Richard Nixon's assistant
during the Watergate scandal. During this trauma, he
told Jeanne he wanted a divorce.

She and John had a wonderful, conventional life
during the years before they left Seattle for Washington, D.C. They married when Jeanne graduated from
college and John was in his second year of law school
in California. She taught school that first year; she
discovered she was pregnant at Christmas and had to
get a special dispensation from the principal to complete the year. As a graduation gift when John finished
law school, his uncle, a well-known Seattle business-
man, invited John and his family to visit Seattle. They
liked it so well that they decided to move there, and
John started a law practice in the city. It was slow
going at first, but John became well-known for some
high-profile environmental cases, among others, and
he started to make a good living. Jeanne was busy
volunteering with a children's theater organization
and the Seattle Symphony. They eventually had five
children.

Then a friend from law school, Bob Haldeman,
asked John to work on Richard Nixon's election campaign. After Nixon's election, John and Jeanne made
a difficult, shared decision for John to accept a job as

one of Nixon's top lawyers. It meant a big reduction in income and a move from the Pacific Northwest, which the whole family loved. But the prospect was exciting, and they would, after all, be coming back home in a few years.

This is Jeanne's story, not John's; his is in the history books. As one of President Nixon's closest advisers, John was deeply implicated in the Watergate scandal and Nixon was forced to fire him. The family went home to Seattle and two years later John was put on trial, convicted, and sent to federal prison. For Jeanne, Watergate meant being spit on in public, trying to keep John from feeling totally defeated when they went back home, and struggling to keep five children fed and clothed without his income. She went back to Washington, D.C., with John for the first trial, but during the second one, she and the children stayed in Seattle. Jeanne returned for the sentencing, and that's when John told her he had been having an affair with her best friend while he was living in Washington during the trial.

She was devastated. She did not want a divorce. She thought John could reestablish himself in Seattle in some way after he served his prison sentence, and she believed the family could and should stay together. So John went to prison and Jeanne stayed home to pick up the pieces. The first Christmas was the hardest, especially on the children. Jeanne was so depressed she was unable to pretend that things were going to be all right. John's uncle and aunt had introduced her to Christian Science, and she found it very helpful. She called her Christian Science practitioner in despair, but instead of sympathy she gave Jeanne a lecture. She asked Jeanne, "What have you done for somebody else today? Get up and do something for someone else."

It was the start of the road back for Jeanne. She got out of bed, mustered strength to comfort her children, and reconnected with the Seattle Symphony program for school children. Volunteering there eventually led to a paying job, and she later opened her own public relations firm. But her marriage was over. When John got out of prison he insisted on the divorce and very soon married another woman who had befriended him when he was in prison.

With a positive outlook and an outgoing personality, Jeanne has made a rewarding life with her second husband, her children, and her grandchildren, though some of the children still nurse scars from that time. Understandably, she sees the move to Washington, D.C., as the cause of the destruction of her first marriage. John was always on call for the president, and that left little time for family. Jeanne believes forgiveness is imperative, and she was able to forgive him. She says, "I couldn't have existed with my children if I had been bitter. They were having a hard time themselves. We stayed good friends, and attended our children's graduations and weddings. But he just couldn't come back."

Increasingly, the women of the Wisdom Trail are facing the prospect of their own or their husbands' failing health. The husbands of Janet Lieberman and Julie Hungar recently died. Nell Berry, Selma Fink, Elaine Hayes, Emily Korzenik, Joyce Millington, and Charlotte Ward are also widows. All of them learned that there is no way to prepare adequately for losing a mate. Several of the women also faced the common precursor: taking care of a mate through a long, terminal illness. Selma Fink uses the experience of caring for her husband during the last years of his life to help other women and men who are facing this difficulty.

To cope with her husband's deteriorating health, Selma drew on the strength of her father's example. As a girl, she lived with the tragedy of her brother's schizophrenia, which diagnosed when he was sixteen years old. She admired her father's approach to the knowledge: "He didn't try to hide it. He took out the encyclopedia and read to us about it. His whole direction was to try to find answers. That had a very profound effect on me, because he took adversity and said, 'What can I do to make it better?'"

Her brother was bright, and he was able to finish high school, but he had unexpected outbursts that were hard to handle. Her father tried everything from counselors to shock treatment without success. Then he was persuaded to allow doctors to perform a prefrontal lobotomy on the boy. It permanently damaged her brother's brain, and the family took care of him until he died in his seventies. Selma says, "My parents felt a sense of responsibility for this son, and they never complained that it was overwhelming, or asked, 'Why did this happen to us?' They taught me that instead of dwelling on the sadness, you think, 'What can I do to make this person's life better?'"

It was a lesson that served her well when her husband developed dementia near the end of his life. She was his caregiver for almost nine years. She finally had to place him in an adult-care residence. One aspect of Selma's wisdom is that she has always looked for and found help when she needed it. During the late stages of her husband's illness, she joined an Alzheimer's support group, and they helped her when she sold the home she had lived in with her husband for many years, moved him to a care facility, then moved to an apartment. Then she felt she needed to move in a more positive direction, and, having learned the value of the support group and wanting to share her experience and encourage others, she created her own small-scale outreach group. Three people meet at her home, and she sees two others regularly. She gives them advice, comfort, and information about resources, goes with them to visit their partners in the care facilities, and reminds them to take care of their own health. She offers herself as a model of what it means to keep going. She also helps other senior citizens to learn techniques in sculpting. As she shares these gifts, she expands her own life.

Although Alice Yee eventually married again after her first husband died, she lived for fifteen years as a single parent. During those years she managed to raise strong children, have a rewarding career, form long-lasting ties with other women, and work through the usual assortment of problems caused by her single status. She had decided not to marry again until her three children were out of the house. She liked to go out with men, but if one began to get serious, she would tell him to look somewhere else. She also learned to be wary of married men who saw a single woman as fair game.

Another hard lesson for Alice was discovering how

difficult it was to buy a home in the days before the women's movement. In 1962, when Alice went to a bank for a mortgage, she found that the state required a man's signature on any mortgage. She had to have a brother or an uncle sign for it. "I had a job, I was an independent head of household, and I refused to accept that." She maneuvered until she got the loan, but she thinks it was only because she was dealing with a local bank in a small town.

Nell Berry never remarried after her husband died. She had two or three opportunities, but she preferred her independent life. In the late 1990s, she received a call from a man who had been a friend of her husband in the service, and with whom she had kept in contact over the years. Both their mates had died, and they both lived in Texas, although he was several hours away. He was going to be in San Antonio, where she lived, and asked her to go to dinner with him. She accepted, and now they see one another frequently, play golf, and go on cruises together. He would like to marry her, but after thirty years of living alone, Nell is not willing to give up her single life. Her Texas spirit comes out when she says, "We're too old for sex and we don't need each other's money. I've never been afraid of being alone. I still have all the social life I desire or need, and I'm comfortable on my own."

One of Alice Yee's most rewarding personal and professional associations was with the Peaceful Valley Group. Unlike Alice, members Jean Phillips, Pat Radcliffe, Mary Jane Stevenson, and Debby Wing never married. Mary Jane has no regrets about not having a family, although she grew up assuming that there wasn't anything to do but get married and raise children. She never met the right person, though, and finally came to the conclusion that she didn't want to have children. "I was afraid of trying to raise them," she says. "My life was complete enough."

For the past sixty years Mary Jane has shared a home with a female colleague from the university. She has been legally blind for over twenty-five years, can read only with magnification, and can't drive. Her housemate, Peg, did all the driving, but the state of her health no longer allows her to drive either. They have moved into two adjacent apartments in a retirement community. Mary Jane resisted the move, but they are both happy there. Together they have a wide circle of friends, including many former students, and are regularly invited to class reunions. They are especially close to a family that lived next door for many years and then urged Mary Jane and Peg to join them in the apartment building. That couple's two children, now grown, are like nieces to the two women.

In addition to these friends, Mary Jane also has a wide network of prominent women leaders throughout the country from her years as dean at Bucknell University. A warm personality, unmistakable sincerity, a caring attitude, and respect for viewpoints other than her own contributed to Mary Jane's success in her career and her valued role in the Peaceful Valley fellowship.

Jean Phillips did not make a conscious choice to stay single either. She thought she might marry a man she went with in college, but realized he wasn't serious about marriage. She wasn't eager to marry either, because her parents' marriage had been pretty unhappy, eventually ending in divorce. After the divorce, her mother had a hard life supporting Jean and her two siblings, and her second marriage didn't end up well either. So, Jean says, "a family wasn't particularly appealing to me unless I found the right person." Working with women's programs in a liberal arts college was totally fulfilling. She enjoyed the students and faculty and felt she had a good life going, so she had no need for a husband.

The close relationships in the Peaceful Valley Group satisfied Jean's need for a place where she could be open and where shared confidences would be kept within the group and not get back to campus. Her only regret is that as a single woman she did not get more socially involved with the faculty at her college. She felt it might be awkward on her own, so she went to a few parties but didn't initiate much other social activity. Since retiring, she has moved from the Midwest to Arizona. She has a housemate and a varied group of friends. She is thoroughly happy with the life she has lived and is living.

Debby Wing doesn't see how people manage to have a career and a family. Her work as dean of women at Knox College was intensely gratifying but also time consuming; she worked long days and often ended up having dinner in the college dining room. She was concerned about her students' welfare, and she worked hard to bring consistency and stability to their life at college. As a result, her job occupied her time fully. She says, "Men left all the household tasks to their wives." She admits knowing women who managed marriage and a career, but she believes she would have found it so difficult that she would probably have given up her career.

Debby's work was not only engrossing; it gave her a rich social life. In addition to being dean, she was also a member of the faculty and taught English courses until her administrative duties became too time consuming. She sees having an active social life as one of the pluses of a career on a college campus. She enjoyed a wide circle of friends on and off campus—married couples and single women and men. She took trips with colleagues in the summers, and in retirement she continues to travel with friends from her working years. In fact, she believes the social aspect of her career has it all over that of many young women today, who spend long hours working on computers in small offices, then going home to husbands and children. She doesn't understand how they have any social life.

Pat Radcliffe's family life influenced her view of marriage, but she didn't understand that when she made the decision to lead a single life. She made her "most important decisions" when a wonderful man who was very much in love with her asked her to marry him and she turned him down. She had always expected to marry and have children, and she thought she was ready to marry him. But when he brought her a diamond, she says, "I was just terrified. I had to say no . . ."

It was a long time before she understood the reasons behind that refusal. She discovered through therapy that she and her siblings had a completely inaccurate picture of their family. "We always thought our parents had the most perfect marriage and our family was simply wonderful. It took me many years to realize it just was not true. We didn't talk. We were a family that didn't talk." She regrets not having had children of her own or the companionship of a husband, and feels that a good marriage would have given her someone to do things with and talk things over with as part of everyday life. Although she has good friends and a full and satisfying life, she sees a different dimension in those pleasures in marriage, and she regrets not having had that. She is still close to two childhood friends, and they travel together and stay in touch often, and, she has the Peaceful Valley group. She says, "I'm surprised how long the list is of people who've been significant in my life."

Pat has had the wisdom to find gratification in serving others. After years working with young college women and building a second career as a clinical therapist, in retirement she has served as vice president of the executive committee for her county's mental health board, is a board member for the Children's Advocacy Center, and does child custody mediation. She also volunteers as a subject for graduate psychological research. Summing up, she says, "My life has been anything but smooth, but I have had wonderful people in my life always. I had to open up and trust."

It took an extra measure of courage for these

women to lead single lives in a world where the great majority of people were couples. They improvised social and work lives that met their needs and they worked in satisfying service professions. Like their peers who married, each of them found her own path on the Wisdom Trail.

FOUR

Motherhood in a Different Register

"The one thing that really changed the behavior of women was the invention of the pill and the availability of contraceptives," says Alice Yee. "Not only because of sexual freedom. Women could now plan a family. They could decide if they were going to have a career. They could decide if they were going to combine career and homemaking. Suddenly they were in charge of their lives."

Most of the Wisdom Trail women married soon after high school or college, unlike today's couples, who may live together for several years before marrying. Engaging in sexual relations before marriage carried a heavy risk in the 1940s. Alice remembers that the fear of getting pregnant was very real. If girls became pregnant in high school, they couldn't finish school. "You were through. It was a terrible disgrace, and the girl was always at fault."

Early marriage, naturally enough, usually led to early pregnancy. It was difficult to prevent. Families with three and four children were common, with encouragement from the magazines popular with women, whose pages lauded the well-managed family of even five or six children and extolled the many time- and work-saving appliances that made that possible. Overpopulation was not an issue in those upbeat days. An efficiency expert's account of the fun and excitement of a really big family was a bestseller in 1946. *Cheaper By the Dozen,* the more or less true story of life in a family of twelve children, was also made into a popular movie.

Another bestseller published that year was Dr. Benjamin Spock's *The Common Sense Book of Baby and Child Care.* Dr. Spock had studied psychoanalysis for six years, an unusual background for a practicing pediatrician. That gave his advice authority for uncertain young parents, whom he advised to trust their instincts rather than the prevailing experts. He told them to feel comfortable picking up babies when they cry, cuddling them, and treating them with affection.

He encouraged allowing children to be individuals and treating them with flexibility rather than rigidity. He said mothers and fathers should enjoy their children.

This was a welcome message, and mothers accepted it eagerly. The norm for child rearing was thus more relaxed than it is today. Child rearing wasn't the fixation it has become. People didn't take their children with them everywhere; they left them with a babysitter when they went out, and neighborhood kids and grandparents did the babysitting. Competitive parenting was not a phenomenon then either. Bragging about one's children overtly was a faux pas. Getting a child into the right preschool was not a determining factor in the success of children, or, by extension, their parents.

Safety was also a less pressing issue, and children had more unorganized and unsupervised time. They walked blocks to school, rode bikes on city streets, and were away from home for long hours on summer days. Now that they're adults, the children of Elaine Hayes love to tell her stories about their adventures as kids. One summer they joined friends who had a big house near Seattle's Lake Washington—and equally adventurous children. While Elaine and Ralph were at work, the kids spent their days at the lake, clinging to floating logs and drifting to the next beach. Fortunately, they didn't drift far out into the lake, and they didn't go through with their plan to swim across it, a distance of nearly five miles across at that point. Janet Lieberman's boys were learning to be independent in Manhattan. They went to school across town, on the West Side of the city. From the time the eldest boy was ten, he and his eight-year-old brother traveled by themselves on the bus.

Parenting was just not the obsession it has become for many mothers today. It was what we did, but it did not define us. The Wisdom Trail women who had children were happy to be parents, and they now enjoy being grandparents. But being a mother is such a common denominator for their generation that they are more interested in talking about what they accomplished beyond raising their families. That is the surprise factor in their lives, the unexpected element.

While sitting at home one day with her three-month-old baby, Alice Dieter asked herself, "'Is this it? Waxing my floor? The neighborhood coffee klatch?' I loved my baby, I thought she was neat, but she didn't have much conversation." So what was life like for the at-home mom? Women of this generation had gone to college in larger numbers than their mothers, some had held responsible jobs before their children were born, then their lives changed. Though they expected to stay at home with their children, sooner or later, energetic and capable women began to resist being tied down. They started asking themselves, "Who am I? What happened to the person I used to be? Can I still use the skills I had?" Carefully, they began to branch out.

But they were not rejecting motherhood. They saw themselves as mothers first, but it wasn't enough for them. They thought they could be more than "just a housewife." They were clear about one thing: Whatever they did needed to have value. They wanted more than just outside activity; they wanted satisfaction. They were driven by a need to exercise their education or talent, or by a sense that they ought to contribute to the community, or by sheer boredom, or all of the above.

These women often started out working for nothing. Alice Dieter wrote stories for the weekly newspaper; Joyce Millington started a soup kitchen for poor schoolchildren; Jeanne Bluechel helped in children's theater; Elaine Hayes led a parent cooperative for inner-city children; June Chen joined the PTA and became a Democratic Party precinct committeewoman; Lorraine Beitler raised money for the children of Biafra; Julie Hungar recruited parents to help desegregate urban schools; Emily Korzenik ran for local office; Selma Fink sculpted. They did these things in their spare time, and more. It was a start.

Alice Dieter says, "I did what seemed right at the moment. I watch my granddaughter, who's rippling with plans, and I worry about her, because if she doesn't do what she's planned, she feels like she's failed." Alice likes Joseph Campbell's saying, "Follow your bliss." That's what these women did. The early volunteering activities weren't conscious steps toward a grander goal; they were simply ways of expanding their lives while being mothers. Each woman moved from those early pursuits to wider horizons as her children grew more independent, persevering even when the next step might take her into uncharted territory.

Elaine Hayes would go from being a parent leader in her children's preschool to director of a federally funded poverty program, her experience recognized even though she only had two years of college. She went on to pioneer the first day care system in her city. Julie Hungar's time volunteering in public schools eventually led her to a post as vice chancellor for a three-campus community college system. Alice Dieter wrote her first columns for nothing, but they led right into her long and successful career as a journalist, not only in print, but also in radio and television. Selma Fink's basement studio became the site of sculpting classes as well as the place where throughout her life she grew as an artist.

Some other mothers didn't wait until their children were in school to start a professional career. Ruth Lubic and Charlotte Ward had embarked on their career paths well before they married. They made it work by forging partnerships with their husbands. It helped that both of the women had careers in fields that gave them some control over their time, as did their husbands. Their relationships were based on sharing, and they persevered through stressful times to make it all work for themselves and their children.

Alice Yee's career and her children's needs did not always mesh smoothly. Twice Alice made decisions that were good for her career but that she knew would be hard on one of her children. She knew the decisions were right for her, she believed that her children could handle the disappointment, and she was confident that the value of keeping the family together outweighed the hardship on one member. Alice had taught school before she was married, but once her first child was born she stopped teaching and stayed home. Then her husband was diagnosed with Hodgkin's disease and given a year to live, and she went back to teaching, at the local community college. Her husband actually lived eight years longer, and soon after he died, she was promoted to dean of students and faculty.

The promotion meant that she reported directly to the college president, so she needed to support his decisions. Alice felt that some of those decisions were ethically questionable from her point of view, and she couldn't stay in the job. It was a dilemma, because she was the breadwinner for herself and her children. Fortunately, she was able to find another position as dean at Central Washington College in Ellensburg, thirty miles away.

Unfortunately, her oldest son was a senior in high school. He understood how important the move was for her, and he urged her to take the job, but he wanted to stay with family friends to finish his senior year at school. Alice said, "No, we go as a family. I know it's hard, but you can adjust." He was crushed, but he later said it was the best thing they ever did. He moved into a small, cliquish high school where he knew no one, and he handled it successfully, so when he went to college, "It was a cinch. I'd already been through it."

A few years later, when her eldest two children were out of high school, Alice moved her family again. This time, her youngest son was a high school senior, and this move was traumatic for him. He remembers it as a very hard year. The redeeming feature was that Alice's new job was at Grinnell, a top-notch liberal arts college in the Midwest that had reciprocal agreements with comparable colleges, which reduced or waived tuition for children of faculty and administrators from partner colleges. When her son was ready for college, he was able to attend another excellent school, one Alice could never have afforded otherwise. She regrets what he went through, but she does not regret her decision. Her four years there during the turmoil of the late sixties were the hardest years of her life, but also the most exciting and stimulating. She was not insensitive to the problems her decisions caused her children, but she expected them to make the best of things.

Alice made another decision for the sake of her children, and it took courage for her. She liked men, and she liked being married. Of the time after her husband's death, she says, "Anyone who has lost a spouse goes through a period of very lonesome years. You've been used to sharing everything with someone very close to you, and now, though you have friends, it's different." But she decided she would not remarry until her children were out of the house. She says, "I did that because we were a very close family. I knew how much energy a full-time, very demanding job, three children, and a lot of activities took. Adding a new husband and all the adjustments—I couldn't do it. I lived fifteen years as a single parent and never regretted it."

She had no doubt that it was the right thing for her family, and she and her children adapted and thrived in the long run. She was able to have it all, eventually. While her children were still at home she met the man who would wait eight years, until she was ready, before they married. They have enjoyed many happy years together since then.

The career decision that caused hardship for Jeanne Bluechel's children was not her own but her husband's. While her first husband, John Ehrlichman, was in law school, she taught school, but she thought her career was over when her first child was born. She would not hold down a job outside the home again until she was left to support her children as a single parent.

Jeanne and her husband wanted a large family, and she loved raising her five children. But she always needed to be active, and she never let her children slow her down. When they were young, she was a busy volunteer, taking leadership roles with a children's theater program and the symphony's family concerts. She says, "I wanted my children to see me doing things in the community, so I didn't have time for everything to be perfect at home. They all had their jobs. I never wanted to make it so easy for them that all they had to do was come home from school and just play. My children knew I loved them dearly, but we were in this together."

When John accepted a job as counsel to President Nixon, the couple knew they would be giving up the family life they loved. They would exchange their pleasant home, their hikes and weekend camping trips, to move to wherever they could find an affordable house outside Washington, D.C. But they thought the children were old enough to handle the change. It would also be difficult financially. John took a big cut in pay, and living in the Washington area was expensive. On a tight budget, Jeanne helped make ends meet by sewing her children's clothes. Despite the sacrifices they anticipated, and with no idea of the coming disaster for John, the move looked like an opportunity that would be foolish to turn down.

The move called on all the skills Jeanne acquired as a child. Having learned to live with poverty then, she knew how to manage their tight finances. The pressures from John's job and his ultimate disgrace were another matter. She believes it completely changed their children's lives, especially their youngest boy. He was only nine when they left Seattle, and he missed having the kind of time with his father that the older children had enjoyed. Sadly for Jeanne, she now has less contact with this son than with her four other children. They suffered less from the absence of their father during the Nixon years and from the trauma of Watergate. She says, "I would never recommend it to people with children."

Parenting is an enterprise fraught with opportunities for making consequential and irrevocable mistakes. Parents look back on things they did and things they failed to do that could have made things better for their children. It is part of the wisdom of Alice Yee and Jeanne Bluechel that they have come to terms with their regrets. It helps that they have lived long enough to develop strong relationships with most of their adult children and with their grandchildren. The time she spends with her sixteen grandchildren is a source of great pleasure for Jeanne today. She will take all of them to the theater, or to the symphony, and then backstage to meet the conductor after the concert. She goes shopping with each of them separately. Alice and her husband have had her grandchildren join them during the summer to camp, fly-fish, and bird-watch in national forest camps. She says they were wonderful years. It's another phase of being a woman that she treasures. "We have a closeness with the grandchildren, who are now in their late twenties and thirties, that we would never have had otherwise."

One of the blessings of grandchildren is that they give people a chance to make up for their shortcomings as parents. Grown children are manifestly grateful for adding to the circle of affection around their children. In truth, we live in an increasingly unsettled society, changing homes and jobs and partners with greater frequency than in the past. As a result, parents of young children today appreciate the extended family grandparents provide. As we give our love to their children they forgive us for old shortcomings.

MANY TRAVELERS ON the Wisdom Trail gave up careers for the sake of their children. June Chen's background marked her for accomplishment. Unusual for their day, her educator parents believed strongly in the importance of educating girls. When she entered National Taiwan University only one woman was enrolled for every ten men there. Nor did June stop learning after her marriage and the couple's move to the United States. Although she worked to provide their income while her husband completed his doctorate, she continued to study mathematics part-time.

The Chens' last stop was in the Pacific Northwest, when June's husband went to work for Boeing. June started college again, but when Boeing offered her a job as well, she accepted it and gave up her studies. She started at the bottom as a key puncher, but soon advanced as she demonstrated increasing computing skills. She kept learning, adding more computer languages, and eventually advanced to a position as a systems analyst. At the time, she was a rarity in her area, both a woman and an Asian.

The work was stimulating. She still enjoys recounting her supervisors' surprise at finding she knew how to wire computers, an important skill in the early days of computing, and one she acquired at a previous job. She worked in business applications, then in scientific applications in the flight-test division. She worked on developing the Boeing 747, and was there to cheer when the first one was rolled out. Her last job was helping to develop the C130 transport for the air force. She loved the changes; she was never interested in maintaining a program after she had developed it, but wanted to move on to something new.

June and her husband very much wanted to have

children, but they were married for sixteen years before she succeeded in getting pregnant. Laughing, she says, "Everybody knows my story. We went to Acapulco, and I learned how to drink mai tai. My second boy—Hawaii!" When her second son was born, June quit her job. She thought it was more important to be at home with her children. But she soon became frustrated without enough outside activity, and made her first foray into politics as a Democratic Party precinct committeewoman. From there, she pursued a busy life of volunteering.

With wide influence in her community and a varied coterie of friends, today June has a full, satisfying life. She is totally dedicated to her family. If you ask her about the future, she says, "The future is my grandson," and quickly offers a picture of a smiling one-year-old. But when you ask about her career, her pride in what she was able to do is tinged with a touch of regret that she quit before knowing how far she might have gone.

Emily Korzenik has said to her children, "You are my greatest enterprise." It's a fitting statement for the Wisdom Trail women, because it puts their desire to achieve in its proper perspective. It honors the primacy of motherhood while recognizing the legitimacy of the other enterprises women engage in.

Indeed, Emily goes on to say, "That didn't mean I couldn't do other things." And she definitely did— from running for the New York State Assembly to earning a master's degree to teaching high school history to becoming a rabbi.

In each of these things, Emily adjusted her life to allay her husband's discomfort with her activities and to make sure she didn't shortchange her children. It was easy to bring them along when she was distributing political signs, but she couldn't take them to class with her when she decided to attend graduate school to prepare for a regular job. So she waited until her youngest child was in kindergarten before she went back for a master's degree. Although she wasn't sure she wanted to be a teacher, she was intent on being more than a bridge-playing matron, and a teacher's schedule meshed with her children's calendar. Even so, a plea from her daughter for more attention helped her realize it would be hard to work full-time, so after she earned her degree she found a part-time position.

After her last child had gone off to college, she made her most significant career move. "I felt the school didn't need me and my children weren't going to need me. It's the only time in my life I was really depressed." That was when she learned of the rabbinical college. Her children were totally in her corner.

When she wavered over the decision, one of her sons asked her, "Have you no sense of adventure?" One of them had tried hang gliding at college, and he told her that for a midlife crisis, hers was better than hang gliding. So she did it. She says for the first time since she got married, she felt free to make a choice that was just for herself.

Julie Hungar remembers her return to college after three years as a housewife. Her husband, definitely progressive where education was concerned, pushed her to finish her master's degree, assuaging her guilt at leaving her preschool children by pointing out that it was like an insurance policy. She loved school, so she didn't need a very big push, but once she enrolled she felt like she was on a seesaw. She was torn every day when her children cried and clung to her skirt as she left them at the babysitter's house. Then she would get to class, thrilled to be in the midst of intellectual discussions, staying afterward to continue the conversations, then tearing herself away reluctantly to pick up her girls.

On the other side of the coin, being a mother often gave women an acceptable entrée to a career. For Julie, being a school volunteer was the first step in her journey to a career in community college education. For Elaine Hayes, joining the parent cooperative preschool for her children was the beginning of a progression from parent leader to instructor to head of the federally funded program creating urban preschools. It was a full-time job, and she accepted it reluctantly because she knew it would take time from her four children. She juggled both roles for five years. Then, she says, "one of my boys started cutting classes too much, and I was getting calls from the school." She would have to take time off from work to go to the high school, find out from his friends where her son was, and make sure he got back to class. So she quit her job at the end of the year. She stayed home until that son was a senior.

Part of parenting wisdom is recognizing that we aren't perfect, that we've done what we can. If our children turn out well, by whatever definition we use, it helps us feel that we didn't do too badly after all. But there is only so much parents can do to protect their children from the outside world. Elaine Hayes only learned when her children were grown how they had been treated when they transferred from a school in the segregated inner city to a majority white school. With one parent who was African American and one who was Japanese American, Elaine's four children had fit in easily at the neighborhood schools in Seattle's Central District, the most racially diverse area of the city. Moving to a majority white school was another story.

When Elaine and her husband moved into their North End home, the children changed schools. For thirteen-year-old Candy, it was hard enough to leave her circle of good friends. She didn't want to move, but she had no choice. At that time Seattle was struggling with school desegregation, and had instituted a voluntary transfer program to encourage students of color to attend majority white schools away from the inner city. As students of color in a North End school, Candy and her brothers were improving racial balance for that school. Candy asked to stay at her old school, which enjoyed a climate of relative harmony in a mixed student body of blacks, white, and Asians. Because of the transfer program, however, there was no way that could happen. What Elaine and Ralph heard from Candy years later was that white kids would stand in the second-floor stairwell of the school and dump buckets of water on her and other transfer students. They learned to ignore the harassing, and Candy eventually formed close friendships that lasted beyond high school.

Elaine doesn't recall doing much, openly at least, to prepare her children for this kind of problem. They knew about the difficulties their father had faced in becoming a schoolteacher. For example, when it came time for Ralph to do the practice teaching required for his education degree, he had a problem: He couldn't find a teacher to supervise his practicum. There was only one African American high school teacher in the public schools, and he didn't teach social science, which was Ralph's subject area. It was a relief for everyone in the family when a woman who taught ninth-grade social studies welcomed him into her classroom and became a mentor. Elaine says, "We never really had a sit-down discussion about this kind of problem, but kids pick up these things." Ralph was eventually hired at one of the city's most multiracial high schools, and he shared stories from school at the dinner table. Problems concerning race in the children's schools were discussed as well. Elaine believes that the combination of tolerance and strength of conviction that she and Ralph demonstrated gave their children the values and skills they needed to face their worlds.

Elaine directly intervened the day her second son, then a seventh-grader, refused to go to school because he had a black eye. He wouldn't explain, so she took him to school and walked into the principal's office with him. The principal asked him what had happened, and her son blurted out, "Nobody's going to call me a nigger or a Jap and get away with it. You have to show guys you aren't going to take that." When the principal gave him a lecture, saying he would just have to get accustomed to things like this and learn how to handle them, Elaine said, "Oh, no, that's not going to happen in any school my kid is going to. It's your job to correct this kind of situation." The principal didn't offer to take action, so Elaine and friends from the PTA organized a program of activities to improve relations among different ethnic groups in the school.

Elaine and Ralph created a supportive and stimulating life for their family. Wherever they lived, they built a network of close friends who shared their view of an open society. At the same time, they fit in well with their neighbors. Elaine says of being an interracial couple, "That never bothered us that much. I knew we were a little different, but we never had an overtly hard time about it." They were good neighbors, mixing well at neighborhood potluck dinners and picnics. Elaine believes they provided a model of how to fit in. They did not seek attention, but their quiet courage showed their children how to make their way.

Of all the challenges Elaine and Ralph met together, the hardest was the death of their daughter.

Candy was forty-three and had been to see a doctor three days in a row, complaining of shortness of breath. The doctor hadn't considered the problem serious enough to check her oxygen level. A day later a blood clot in her lung caused her death. Three years later, Elaine lost Ralph, again after physicians failed to diagnose his condition properly. In recounting these events, Elaine gives the barest facts without expressing whatever bitterness she may harbor. She has been buoyed by her three sons and their families, her wide group of friends, and her many interests.

Alice Dieter lost a child too, early in her married life. He was her second child, the first boy, and he lived just thirty-one days. He had been fine until the night they found that he had stopped breathing, and her husband rushed him to the hospital. The autopsy showed that he had fulminating pneumonia, and the doctors said they wouldn't have known he was sick even if he had been in the hospital. Alice feared that because the baby had been without oxygen he would be severely damaged if the doctors succeeded in reviving him, and she thought, "I can't deal with that."

She got pregnant again right away and bore another son; later she had one more boy. The older son had severe dyslexia, at a time when the condition was not recognized. She says, "His childhood was extremely trying for all of us. He's a great guy, but his life has been really hard. I learned that you can't say 'I can't.' It reinforced my feeling that you live well with what you have at the moment. My baby's death did not make me fearful, and it didn't make me bitter." She did experience guilt, though. She had not enjoyed breast-feeding her first child, and had given it up after five weeks. She didn't breast-feed her second child, and she wondered if it would have protected him from the pneumonia. Actually, breast-feeding was much less common among Alice's generation of mothers than it is today. She notes the contrast with her daughter, who breast-fed both her children until they were old enough to come and ask for it.

Alice's sorrow as a parent is not about the son who died but about the one with dyslexia, whose needs she believes she failed to meet. She says, "On the one hand I was the mother who fought for him and never gave up, who wouldn't let the system put him in the wrong box. On the other hand, I wasn't the mother with patience and calmness. I remember chasing him up the stairs and saying, 'You've got to control yourself,' totally out of control myself, setting a marvelous example with fireworks in every direction." The trauma of her son's childhood, she thinks, affected his sister as well, and both of them have struggled as adults. The life of her youngest son has been less fraught than that of his older siblings, and Alice has a gratifying relationship as a grandmother to his son, as well as to her daughter's girls. She is clear-eyed about where she failed her children, but she is still hopeful for them. She says, "You can't replay the story."

Life as a mother is not a rose garden, even on the Wisdom Trail. That can be said of every generation. In fact, several of our women who never married attribute their decision at least in part to their childhood in unhappy families and the resulting conscious or unconscious choice not to take on the responsibility of raising children. They have found other ways to have caring relationships, and have met their need to nurture through careers involving young people, and by being close to the children of their family and friends.

For those who were mothers, their lifelong challenge has been to emphasize the joys that children bring while coping with disappointment and regret. The qualities that mark our women are shared by the many other women who have reached their seventh or eighth decade alive and well and still knowing love, even though they may have lost the men with whom they had children. They have kept up their courage when things went wrong or when it seemed impossible to live the full life they craved. They maintain connections with their children and grandchildren and with their friends, and they keep giving back to their community as volunteers. They have adapted to the tragedies and blessings that have come along, and to the needs and desires of their husbands and children. They have improvised ways to be good mothers and also to have a life for themselves, and today they recognize that their children and grandchildren are their greatest legacy and their greatest joy.

There's no getting away from it: Regardless of what else has been important in their lives, the grandmothers of the Wisdom Trail, like grandmothers everywhere, find a different kind and level of satisfaction in their children's children. Beyond the opportunity to help one's children and to make up for parenting mistakes, and regardless of one's religious beliefs, grandchildren are our visible legacy. June Chen says it well: "The future is my grandson." We see in them a mixture of ourselves, our mates, and our children, and we see the new challenges and opportunities they will meet with our combined heritage.

FIVE

Beyond the Comfort Zone

American society has changed immeasurably since the Wisdom Trail women were young. They couldn't have imagined when they were starting families and careers in the 1940s and 1950s how different women's lives would be only a half century later. Without planning to reject the patterns of their mothers' generation, their journeys turned out to be at the forefront of those changes. What led them to strike out in directions that were unusual in their time but that have now become commonplace? The rush to reestablish what had been normal life in the early years after World War II reinforced the narrowness of women's role. But at the same time, another current was moving the country in a more expansive direction. The end of the war had given Americans a great sense of confidence about their role in the world. It led to the Marshall Plan, the generous measure that helped devastated countries recover from the war. Foreign aid programs expanded. The horrors of the Holocaust focused attention on the need for tolerance and equality. President Harry Truman's desegregation of the military late in the war planted the idea that much needed to be done to create an egalitarian society. Prosperity and comfort were increasing as a result of the nation's manufacturing power and ingenuity, supported by an increasingly educated populace, thanks in part to the GI Bill.

These and other factors stimulated an exhilarating sense of possibility in the nation. The seeds of the women's movement of the sixties and seventies were found in the wartime feats of Rosie the Riveter and her coworkers, and the growing number of women going to college. Reflecting the subtle influence of these currents, women like those on the Wisdom Trail were pioneers, more attuned than most to the emerging spirit of the time.

The truth is, though, that most of them didn't have pioneering in mind. They weren't into marching or calling attention to themselves. In fact, for them the less attention paid to them, the better. They were happy to slip under the social radar. All they wanted was to find an outlet for their energy, education, and talent. Because of their grounding in the traditional role of women, they sought outlets with a social purpose, enterprises that addressed a social need. They looked for something that fit that bill and that also matched their capabilities and circumstances. They didn't have their eyes on a bigger prize than that. Without explicitly setting out to make their mark on the world, they found opportunities to amplify their skills and experiences as they kept their families intact in ways that gave them more time and energy. Coming of age in a culture that didn't expect anything of women beyond being a housewife and mother, they thought anything more than that would be fine. And it was, in the beginning. But they carried the seed of greater things.

Because they didn't see themselves as being on an exalted quest and didn't need to impress others, they made their moves without alienating their peers. The women on the Wisdom Trail found new friends among other women who had similar goals, and whose intensity matched their own. That didn't mean they gave up old friends who chose to stay within the conventional cocoon. For the most part, other women were encouraging. They came to the fundraisers and traded babysitting, but while one woman used that free time to volunteer at her local school or go back to college, her neighbor might use it for a few hours at the outlet mall. (Yes, they had outlet malls in those days.)

Women who chose this path sometimes paid a price. Conventions die hard, and families, friends, or people who felt their authority was threatened could present a challenge. When Sister Madonna Buder took up marathon running, she knew the sisters in her order didn't consider that an appropriate activity for a nun, and she wasn't sure what her bishop would think of it either. She says, "I didn't want to be a scandal to the church," so she decided to get the bishop's permission. When she met with him, she told him, "I want to inform you of my intention to run the Boston Marathon to collect funds for multiple sclerosis, and I thought you should know about it in case there's any flak." The bishop sat back in his chair and said, "Sister, I wish some of my priests would do what you're doing." That was all, and it was all she needed. He would be prepared in case her picture popped up in the news. She felt isolated from her sisters, who made it clear that they didn't approve, but she didn't let that bother her. Her attitude was shaped by a message she heard on a retreat and adopted as her response to critics: "You do not have to apologize for the gifts that are given you. The only thing you have to apologize for is not using what God has given you as a credit to His glory."

Of course, Sister Madonna's name has been in the news ever since, but she never received any criticism from the bishop. Besides her unusual hobby for a nun, she has been the object of attention because of her age. She was over fifty when she ran her first marathon, and she's still running and looking good in her late seventies. She thrives on what she is able to do and on the attention she garners for her achievements. It takes the sting out of the disapproval of her peers.

Intellectual trailblazing is Janet Lieberman's forte. Early in her career as an educator, she saw the high drop-out rate of high school students in large urban school systems as a terrible waste of human potential. She knew it was over 30 percent in New York City, although school authorities didn't admit it. It was her idea to set up a high school on a college campus for students whose behavior patterns included predictors of failure: long-term absence; evidence of emotional disturbance in the home; reading problems; and poor grades. She believed going to school on a college campus would motivate these students as they saw others from a similar background succeed in higher education.

That was the germ for Middle College High School, started on the campus of LaGuardia Community College in Queens. The idea would spread to more than thirty schools throughout the country, but before it ever got off the ground, Janet had to fight some battles. The president of her college told her that what she wanted to do was impossible, but he didn't try to stop her. To make it happen she had to solve the problems involved in bringing together two separate educational systems. Educational bureaucracies resisted crossing institutional lines to combine high school with college. Janet had to sell her idea to everyone in authority in the educational universe: the superintendent of schools; the chancellor of the City University of New York; the New York State Board of Regents; and finally, the governor. Along the way she realized that the problem had nothing to do with what was taught and everything to do with how the money would be distributed.

With the success of Middle College under her belt, Janet faced fewer obstacles with her next idea, a school for second-language students operating on the same principles: a challenging academic program; small classes; and individualized programs. She had seen capable students fail because they were not able to make the transition from their bilingual middle-school education to high school classes taught entirely in English. She designed a model that took students in the lowest quartile in English proficiency and enabled them to succeed in an all-English program.

Then she took on another challenge. This time, it was providing community college students with an introduction to the kind of education they would never have the opportunity to experience on their own. Working with creative administrators from Vassar, she helped eradicate some of the obstacles to higher education for the underprivileged by instituting a rigorous summer program for community college students at Ivy League colleges. She had to overcome the skepticism of faculty in both institutions and find the funds to make her vision possible. The resulting program has raised the aspirations and degree attainment of hundreds of underprivileged students and created opportunities for immigrant and poor students to get the education they need to succeed.

Elaine Ishikawa was not thinking about pioneering when she accepted Ralph Hayes's invitation to go to a movie. They were having coffee with other staff members of the American Council on Race Relations in Chicago when Ralph made an open invitation to the movies. Elaine said she would go with him. A Japanese American woman dating an African American man didn't seem unusual in the diversity-friendly office of the American Council, but it was not the norm in Chicago in 1948. When they married, Elaine and Ralph had to overcome cultural differences and a bias against interracial marriage in society at large and in their ethnic groups.

Elaine knew better than to bring Ralph to the Presbyterian church her family attended, but she did invite him to the church youth group she worked with. One day the minister came to one of the meetings and spotted Ralph. He asked Elaine who Ralph was, and when she said he was her boyfriend, the minister told her she should not be seeing him. Every Sunday, the minister told her not to continue dating Ralph. Finally, when she wouldn't back down, he asked for a meeting with her mother, and told her his views on Elaine's choice. Her mother asked if he had ever talked to Ralph. The minister said no. She replied, "You should get to know him. He's a very intelligent person."

That ended the minister's campaign, and Elaine and Ralph were married a couple of years later. It was not the last of many challenges the Hayeses would face in the early years of their marriage. They didn't talk much about it. Elaine says, "We knew we were different, but it never bothered us much." Both of them had dealt with obstacles before, so they were adept at overcoming them. Elaine had experienced life in an internment camp, and had survived on her own in Chicago; she was a talented and resourceful improviser.

She minimized overt racism by seeking people and organizations that were progressive in matters of race. When she moved to Seattle, where Ralph went to finish college, she took a room at the YWCA. She had been active in the Y in California as a girl, and she knew the organization was relatively unbiased. Still, she took the precaution of writing ahead that she was seeing a young Negro man, and needed to know if that would be a problem before she made a reservation.

Elaine found a job with the American Friends Service Committee, which she knew had been sympathetic to Japanese Americans in the internment camps. Another of her discoveries was a small, integrated, and socially conscious church. She and Ralph found a warm welcome there, and members of the congregation became their extended family. They were married there, and when the church closed, they moved with other members to a nearby Unitarian Church, another liberal congregation.

Wherever they went the Hayeses made a full social life, from the comfortable and racially mixed neighborhood where they lived when their children were young to their eventual home in a white enclave in the city's North End. Elaine admits, however, that she and Ralph experienced what she will only call "complications." Several incidents involved prejudice from Japanese Americans. There were complaints from some white parents when Elaine joined the PTA board at Roosevelt, the majority white high school her children attended, but Elaine and the PTA ignored them.

One of these complications, which she and Ralph only understood long afterward, almost kept them from moving to the North End. They were buying a big, wonderful house from some friends, and had given the bank a five-thousand-dollar check as earnest money for the purchase. The bank returned the check and refused to grant the mortgage. After several months their friends were able to convince another bank to make the loan, and Elaine and Ralph moved in with their four children. Fifteen years later, by then thoroughly integrated into the community, Elaine learned that after they made the down payment one of their neighbors had circulated a petition, signed by many who were now their good neighbors, opposing the Hayeses' move into the neighborhood. That was why the bank had turned down their application.

Like other women of the Wisdom Trail, Elaine is not bitter or regretful as she recounts these experiences. They are trail markers, signs of her ability to integrate the negatives, learn from disappointments, and keep moving forward.

For women on the Wisdom Trail, living out in front of the pack has been an unintended consequence of following their own bent. Discovering that they were "a little different," as Elaine Hayes says, these quiet trailblazers looked for balance, tried to be diplomatic and not openly defiant of conventions, yet stood firm when necessary. It's a combination of skills that is characteristic of women achievers. They demonstrated how to push boundaries and expand horizons while being tactful, considerate, and strong.

Strength is a necessity for women who choose to address important social problems. Our nation's history is filled with stories of women who exercised their will to make positive change. Society women of the 1890s who opposed killing birds for use by the hat industry led the Audubon Society to become a nationwide conservation organization. Women's organizations fought for the passage of the Nineteenth Amendment. Our women followed their example. Ruth Lubic challenged the medical profession to force acceptance of her birthing centers as a means of reducing high infant mortality rates among the poor. She forced members of Congress to address this problem where it is most severe, in our capital city. She pushed insurance companies to recognize the human value and the efficiency of her clinics. Likewise, Emily Korzenik challenged the insular political system in her comfortable suburb, and Charlotte Ward faced down the academic establishment's bias against women in science.

Claudia Thomas challenged people who denied access to women and people of color. Claudia's mother, a businesswoman, taught her children that people are people no matter what color they are, and that it's their behavior you have to be concerned with. After her first job at *Ebony* magazine, she taught school. When they moved to Lakewood, near her husband's post at Fort Lewis, Washington, Claudia taught again. She earned tenure and had good evaluations. Then she applied for a vice principal's position. Parents of some of her students were on the screening committee; they told her that her application had been discarded without a review. Claudia immediately filed suit in two jurisdictions, state and federal, on the basis of gender discrimination. The district's record of hiring women in administrative positions was as dismal as it was for hiring people of color.

The local media took up the story, and their big question was how much money Claudia expected to get from the suit. She told them, "I'm not asking for money. I've been working since I was six years old, and I work for what I get. I'm asking the school district to do what is right. I don't need this job. I love working with kids, so I don't care if I'm never an administrator. But I'm going to hold this district accountable, or they will never get any federal funds."

The district settled by offering her the job. Before she would accept it, she told the superintendent and the board to look at all the applications, including her own, and decide who was best qualified. When the board did, they told the superintendent that Claudia was clearly the top person. He offered to hire her for a probationary period. She challenged him to name any male appointees he had hired on that basis. Her lawyer got the board members on the telephone, and they directed the superintendent to hire her with no strings attached. That didn't end the foot-dragging, but eventually she won his support. A few years later, when she had become a principal, the superintendent praised her as a model to other principals in the district.

Many of our women who had the confidence to challenge authority or convention and succeeded in expanding horizons for everyone give credit to family influences for their strength. Like Claudia, Sister Madonna was her grandfather's darling. She was the first grandchild and initially a great disappointment to her German grandfather, who had demanded a grandson to carry on the family name. But when Madonna was an infant, she charmed him and became his little princess. By the time the first of three brothers came along, she says with a laugh, she had already established her preeminence. Charlotte Ward also profited from the approval and intellectual stimulation offered by her uncle; she is another woman who cites the early support of a male authority figure as significant to her development.

Claudia credits both her mother and her grandfather as strong influences. Charlotte's three aunts as well as her uncle were sources of strength. Elaine Hayes's mother was an extremely capable businesswoman and very open-minded. Elaine knew that her grandfather was a samurai, a member of an elite warrior class in Japan, but she didn't know that it meant anything special. Her mother was interested in democracy and women's rights, and she did not pass on Japanese class consciousness to her children. Elaine's role model was a progressive and independent woman who gave her daughters the spunk and courage to carve a different path for themselves when they grew up.

As we've seen, Janet Lieberman had a different influence—benign neglect. She was well loved but never got much attention, so she was free to develop on her own terms. Claudia, Janet, and Elaine say these positive influences explain their confidence in facing opposition and persevering to overcome obstacles.

Many women of the Wisdom Trail see adversity as contributing to their strength. For them, as for people in every age, adversity was a crucible that helped forge their strong will in spite of the odds. Adversity comes in many forms. Although the spirit of the nation after World War II was strong, it was definitely not so during the Depression, when these women were in their formative years. Many of them were poor, and the ways their families dealt with poverty made an indelible mark. Alice Yee remembers when her father worked for the WPA, and her mother made her children's clothes. Alice recalls the thrill she felt when her aunt gave her and her sister their first "boughten" dresses in high school. Formed by years spent picking fruit and vegetables for canning, Alice still picks tomatoes and peppers for pickles and relishes, and dries pears and apples when harvest season comes. "I was a child of the Depression. It took years before I could spend a dime and not agonize over whether I could afford it." The power that comes from knowing you can make do in hard times gave her the strength to adapt when her husband died and hard times came again.

Lorraine Beitler was influenced by the adversity her parents surmounted when they came to this country. She was grateful to them and she integrated their values, including the importance of hard work and education. She was the first in her family to go to college; she traveled two hours each way by train. She says, "For an eight o'clock lab I had to be up at five, on the train by six. It was pitch dark. I was scared sometimes. I got a corner seat on the same car each day, and I would tuck my books under the seat and go to sleep. The conductor would always wake me up in time to change for the local train." She wanted to study art but knew she should study something that would lead to a job, so she chose chemistry.

Then as now, clothing was a significant factor for young girls. Julie Hungar's town wasn't as sophisticated at Lorraine's, so it was sweaters with a Jantzen label, not cashmeres, that were the object of desire. In high school the clothes Julie's mother made were always a little different from what everyone else was wearing, and she could never afford the right sweater. Unlike most girls in her town, Julie had been brought up expecting to go to college, but with three younger children to support, her parents didn't have the money to pay her way. So after finishing high school, she stayed home, went to the junior college, and worked for two years to earn money for the university. As soon as she had enough of her own money, one happy day she bought herself a Jantzen sweater. It was a first step on the road to earning an independent income when she was a married woman.

Alice Dieter remembers her folks as "dirt poor." They were farmers, so they had plenty to eat, but no money. She recognizes her relative good fortune. "I'm glad now that I experienced the Depression without experiencing real denial." That's typical of our women who grew up poor: They remember the poverty, but the sting is long gone, and their memories of childhood are pleasant. Even Jeanne Bluechel is grateful that her mother somehow afforded to have music in her life. The positive and negative lessons from her childhood forged the sunny personality she has as an adult.

Emily Korzenik recognizes adversity in her childhood, but from the vantage point of almost eighty years she believes the good outweighed the bad. "I feel how tremendously fortunate my whole life has been. I had all the advantages of parents who adored their children." There was a downside: Her parents bickered constantly with each other, which forced young Emily into a leadership role. Had they lived today, she believes they would have divorced, but in those days that wasn't acceptable for a middle-class Jewish family. The upside was that as family mediator Emily developed maturity beyond her years.

Patricia Radcliffe's life direction was also affected by how unhappily married her parents were. She attributes her decision not to marry the man who loved her to the undercurrent of unhappiness in her parents' unhappy marriage, but she recognizes the value of the lessons she learned. "The difficulties I've had are a really important part of my life. They've added richness, as painful as they were. The whole process of recovery [from alcoholism] and personal growth in therapy made it possible for me to have a really good life today."

Childhood in an unhappy family is also the reason Jean Phillips stayed single. "My family was not a happy family. I had probably seen almost the worst of family life." Her father, who went into the navy during the war, was more interested in the ocean than in his family. Jean remembers that he bought himself a speedboat, but she says, "It was his toy. I think I got a ride in it once." Her parents divorced about the time the war began, and her mother had to support her three children. Jean's mother found work at the docks in Gloucester, Massachusetts, cleaning fish, although she later got a secretarial job. Jean knew what it was like to struggle and persevere, and it contributed to her self-reliance as an adult.

Each of the women who experienced adversity early in life looks at it now as a source of wisdom. The hard times they lived through have helped them to cope with the ups and downs that come to everyone. They see the sum of their lives as fortunate, having lived long enough to profit from mastering adversity.

There is a downside to a long life: growing old. In giving credit to aging for the lessons acquired through living, it's only fair to look at the double nature of this gift. Everyone in her seventies and eighties, with the possible exception of Sister Madonna, is aware of physical, mental, and spiritual losses. The joints deteriorate, the constitution weakens, vision and hearing fail. Memory doesn't serve as readily as it once did. At least since the middle of the last century, American culture has notoriously been focused on youth. Fashions in body type, clothing, and entertainment all favor young people, and the pervasiveness of technology has left many feeling confused or completely shut off from the world. With all the problems in the world and in our country's place in it, it's tempting to look back with nostalgia and feel that, along with ourselves, our country may be past its prime.

On the plus side, having lived at least three-quarters of a century, the women of the Wisdom Trail are deeply aware of their good fortune. They have lived through the Depression, World War II, and several subsequent wars; they have seen the successful battle for civil rights; and they have enjoyed the benefits of the women's movement. They understand themselves and their world better, and they are surer of their values and their own worth. They have been able to live by their own principles and pursue satisfying efforts to solve societal problems. Although it didn't occur to them that the way they lived would be helpful to anyone in the future, the women of the Wisdom Trail embody for later generations a brand of wisdom forged by life in a time of cataclysmic change in women's roles.

Their generation shows signs of coming into its own. The media are full of stories about healthy, successful older women and men who have benefited from nutritious food, good medical care, exercise, and avoiding abuse of their bodies. The women of the

Wisdom Trail accept the realities of aging without feeling the need to use Botox or liposuction. Younger people are recognizing the value of elders as role models, especially women. The middle generation of women with aspirations has discovered the difficulties of prioritizing marriage, children, career, and quality of life. To make good decisions for themselves, many have looked for guidance to their predecessors, the pioneers who have already made those decisions. It's gratifying to our women.

When Julie Hungar became the first woman to serve on the executive cabinet of her community college district, she did not foresee that she would become a role model. During her eleven challenging years in that position, for which she later realized she had been drastically unprepared, she learned to overcome the obstacles and became an example to younger women in the system. That was the last thing on her mind; for most of those years she was scrambling to keep her job.

Julie's first challenge came from a quarter she did not anticipate: the college faculty. She had been a faculty member at Seattle Central Community College for ten years, was an officer in the faculty union, and sat on the faculty side at the collective bargaining table. When the president appointed her chair of her large academic division, it put her on the side of the administration. She worked hard to gain her colleagues' acceptance through her collegial leadership style, and thought she had succeeded. Then the college president was made district chancellor for the three-college Seattle district, and he appointed Julie vice chancellor for education for the district. A vigilant union grievance officer protested that she was not selected through an open process. The position was advertised, and Julie got the job. But she was off on the wrong foot from the start.

Because she had once been an active member of the faculty union, Julie was also resented by college administrators who considered union members adversaries. They also resisted interference from district headquarters in their college's programs. She responded by making the job one of persuasion and group process, and collaborated with the college vice presidents on instruction and student services. She survived the arrival and departure of five chancellors during her tenure.

Keeping her job and her sanity in this position called for adapting, persevering, and developing new skills. But Julie retired with good friends and supporters on all three campuses—faculty, staff, and administrators. Women administrators and staff members told her she had been a model for them, as one of the few women in a leadership position. She earned the satisfaction that comes from living long enough to feel you have met the challenges of your career, earned respect and regard, and won over and forgiven your enemies. If you also have family and friends to brighten your life, life is good.

Another milepost on the Wisdom Trail is the recognition that the well-lived life is constantly changing and bringing new growth. This continuing discovery of new ways to expand keeps surprising us as we grow old and have to accommodate declining faculties and energy. We must adapt and persevere; this is no time to give up.

Joyce Millington has had to do more adapting than most, but she is a prime example of how to do it. She moved to a new country late in life and adapted to a new culture, and then adjusted to a change from a life of comfort and respect to one in which she knew no one and had to work hard for a living. In her Trinidad home, she was the wife of a business executive and clergyman. She could afford to do her community work, help poor families privately, and enlist women from her church group in her projects.

Then Joyce's husband lost most of his money through the failure of a financial institution in Trinidad. He began to lose his eyesight, so they came to the United States for eye surgery. Sadly, it made her husband's vision worse. Their children were living in New York City, so Joyce and her husband moved there permanently. That changed almost every aspect of Joyce's life. Her husband became ill and passed away, she lost the community where she was known and had position, and in her new home she was often treated with disrespect because of the color of her skin and her Trinidadian-British accent.

With only a small pension from Trinidad and her work as a babysitter, Joyce was less able to help others than she had been at home. But she found a church in the city where she could preach, and also discovered a place where she could help. She saw young people, especially boys, who were living on the street, and she would give them a little money and advice about where they could go for help. She is not afraid to intervene when she sees them in trouble with the police or in fights. She tells the teenagers that it's better to "negotiate" than fight, and employs her skill to settle arguments on the street. Her children worry about her; what she does is not the usual way in the city. But her confidence in her ability to convince has been borne out by successful interventions. Joyce has found a new way to carry out one of her purposes.

She also takes community college classes and may try to complete a degree. Above all, she says, "I stay cheerful. I'm lucky in that."

Patricia Radcliffe never married and had a family, but her life has been nurturing. After two successful careers, she has expanded in new directions. She uses her professional and administrative expertise as a volunteer for several organizations that address community needs. She is vice president of the executive committee for her community's mental health board, and is on the board of the Children's Advocacy Center, which provides support for abused children.

Her most gratifying activity is her work in child custody mediation with divorcing couples. She says, "When one is successful and the parents come up with a parenting agreement they can both live with and that is reasonable for the children, that feels really good. Making a difference for others is a theme for me." Patricia does things for herself, too—another key to living well while living long. When she was sixty-seven, she took up singing lessons, and she sings in three choruses in her city. She sings in German, Latin, Greek, and French. "I surprise myself." But she notes that she has always enjoyed learning new things. She continues to volunteer for graduate students' research projects. That, she says, "is such fun, and it's giving back a little, because I was given a lot."

VISTAS ARE CONSTANTLY unfolding on the route of the Wisdom Trail. As its travelers savor the good parts of the road they've passed, they also look at the possibilities on the road ahead. They are still pioneering, but now in exploring new ways to enjoy growing old. Adversity doesn't frighten them, because they've seen it before and they've coped. They are still courageous, even more willing to speak up to power because they are secure in themselves. Their courage helps them face the obstacles they know they cannot overcome—the loss and the deterioration that come with aging.

SIX

The Legacy of the Wisdom Trail

From girdles and aprons to bikinis and bodysuits, and from being at the back of the line to leading the parade, women have gone from a face in the crowd to winners in a multitude of contests. How did it happen?

If there's a secret to the well-lived life along the Wisdom Trail, it is in attitudes, not in platitudes. With all they've attained, the women whose paths we have followed are still busy living, pursuing avenues new and old. Dispensing "Rules for Living Well" is not what they do. They offer stories rather than answers. In unheralded ways, they have significantly improved the world we live in. The essence of the trail is in the details of their lives and the qualities that distinguish them. Their achievements are seminal.

We look to their lives to harvest the wisdom in them. How have these women managed their lives? What memorable decisions did they make that are possible for others to follow? What common elements on their individual paths stand out as mileposts on the trail? What does the trail look like to them as they reflect back on it and look forward to the future?

Their stories are about connection, a first principle for all those on the Wisdom Trail. They speak eloquently of what connection to their birth family meant. Although their parents' influence wasn't always positive, they are grateful for the gifts of their upbringing. As parents and grandparents themselves, they have gained an understanding of the difficulties of raising children and the strains their parents lived under while raising them. It is a pleasure for them to look back and relive their early family connections. Remembering that they sometimes resented heavy-handed advice from parents and in-laws, they usually zip their lips when their impulse is to correct modern child-rearing practices.

Then the storytellers focus on the life connections they made as adults: with husbands if they were married, or with other women and men if they were not. There is a sense of freedom in the relationships of the never married that is less common in those who lived with men. The single women did not experience the tension that many wives felt, the feeling of being torn between what their men wanted and expected of them and what they wanted and expected of themselves. The relationships the single women developed were usually supportive, and their recollections lack the push and pull of competing interests. They had only their own direction to pursue, and close friends met their needs for advice, encouragement, and connection.

Some of these women feel a twinge of regret for missing the marriage and family scene. True, the norms when they were at marrying age programmed them for regret. Today women and men are less constrained by societal expectations of marriage and family. But this does not seem to have significantly diminished the sense among women that they are missing something important if they don't have children.

Among our women who married those who truly had it all are the ones who have been completely equal partners. A marriage of equals was natural to them. Those with a strong sense of direction or a college degree in the field they wanted to pursue had a combination of confidence in their own intentions and a commitment to the partnership that enabled them to start out on their way securely in tandem.

The majority of our wives, though, started married life committed to the partnership but less certain about their own direction. Yet they harbored expectations. Whatever combination of factors influenced them—family values, admired role models, movements in the zeitgeist—they sensed the inequities in society and wanted to make the world a better place. They were driven to capitalize on their education and skill and to be of service to others. Their husbands' attitudes were a mixed bag, though they don't recount fierce battles or ultimatums that stopped them in their tracks. But they certainly faced discouragement, ranging from indifference to outright hostility, as they took up priorities beyond home life.

Perhaps that is why they didn't make plans. They may not have admitted even to themselves how far they might go. But they proved that you can go a long way without a plan. They started small, volunteering for an organization whose goals they shared, taking a part-time job when their children were in school, or continuing their education to keep their minds alive. They adopted an attitude of compromise and adaptation to do their own thing while keeping their family life together. They ultimately achieved greater balance in the partnership by educating their partners in increments to accept that their wives were not ordinary June Cleavers.

Compromise kept some of them from pursuing a desired goal. This was done consciously, by weighing the consequences and deciding how much they would give up for the sake of family. Some chose not to have careers while others just moved ahead. Today, fully aware of the roads not taken, these women are nevertheless well satisfied with the trade-offs they made. They made their marriages work, they raised children who are for the most part doing well as adults, and they found a way to volunteer and accomplish goals that were worthwhile to them and to the world around them.

The grandchild factor adds to this feeling of satisfaction in some women's lives. They get intense gratification from seeing their children's children grow up. It is a joy compounded, because it brings about a new and deeper relationship with another generation. Young parents today are perhaps more aware than earlier generations of how important an extended family is for their children, and they are grateful when they see women of the Wisdom Trail enjoy and connect with their children. Keeping the circle of generations together can be harder in today's nomadic society, as distance often rules out the special Friday night dinners with the whole family. Fortunately, travel is more accessible than it was fifty years ago. Older women cheerfully fly to visit their far-flung children or friends' children, who are happy to have their own children hear the old stories of "in my days." Women who never married enjoy mentoring and guiding other family members and students from the past.

Contribution shares nearly equal billing with connection on the Wisdom Trail. It is the urge that called these women to break out of the conventional mode. Most of them found a profession that would allow them to solve community problems and get paid for their work. Others made their contribution as volunteers, but in high-impact positions. Although largely unheralded, they have changed their communities and sometimes altered the bigger picture. Not surprisingly, a major area of effort has been education, from preschool level to university. They have been teachers, but they have been much more. They have initiated educational methods and programs, influenced school systems, and pressured public officials to allow them to carry out their educational innovations.

Some of our women fought bias against women and

people of color, promoted the importance of justice and ethics in opposing anti-Semitism, ran for political office, and led the battle for better health care for mothers and children in poverty. They have given the gift of creative expression to blind people and cancer patients, helped troubled girls develop into successful adults, brought music to inner-city children, and counseled families involved in the juvenile system. American arts and the reading public have benefited from their work with public institutions.

Why have they done it? What was the rationale and reward? As they tell it, the answers are pretty prosaic. They are all quite modest about what they've done and why. None of them had visions of grandeur; they were not ambitious and did not seek power or glory. Their ambition was to achieve something worthwhile with whatever talent they had, to work on a problem that interested them and that they believed was important. The reward has been intense personal satisfaction and the knowledge that they have done something that mattered. Those who were paid for their work had the additional gratification of knowing that society placed a value on their activities. Those who were volunteers are aware of missing that concrete recognition, but they are no less satisfied or proud of what they contributed. The sheer pleasure of knowing that they made a difference is enough for them.

As the women reflect on their lives, these two elements are central: the world's work they have done, and their life among family and friends. Their significant decisions have all been related to these two things, and a big part for them has been how to maintain the balance between the two. The juggling act between the connected life and the contributing life is a major theme. Lots of daily decisions call for trade-offs: Do I skip the conference or miss my daughter's field hockey game? Is it the first time she will be on the starting team? Can someone else in the office represent us as well at the conference? If I attend the conference, can I make it up to my daughter some other way? Every choice has its cost. When it is for contribution rather than connection, or for work instead of family, the price is a residue of guilt.

On the other hand, when the choice was for family over career, it was a sacrifice of opportunities. The women of the Wisdom Trail have often made decisions that meant giving up potential careers or more significant influence, not to mention recognition, in favor of their families. They alleviated their disappointment by pursuing directions that were compatible with their children's needs or their husbands' comfort level, but that still gave them opportunities to make gratifying contributions.

But none of them has a magic formula for sustaining connection and contribution, and they have concentrated on finding the best possible balance between the two. They accept regrets and guilt as the cost of taking responsibility for living a full life.

Our travelers discovered motivating aspects along the trail. As the women's movement grew and matured around them, they found themselves in the vanguard. Success helped them build confidence as they realized that they were in the first significant cohort of two-career families and they were making it work. They began to recognize their power as mentors for other women and to realize the pleasure of finding others with similar aspirations. For some it was a revelation to discover that they liked and worked well with other women. The old stereotype was that women couldn't get along with each other. With increasing confidence, these women discovered this was no more true than the misperception that they couldn't work well with men. Categories of easy and difficult among coworkers knew no gender. As they age, the women of the Wisdom Trail appreciate the value of mentoring. Although they were examples to younger women just by living their lives, and as a group offered silent models of accomplishment, sometimes it involved overt action: recommending younger women for promotion, helping them to see opportunities, and bolstering their self-confidence.

Many of them became role models for their own children. A special pleasure has been helping their children mature with a sense that the future is wide open, that as young men and women there are no limits to what they can do with their lives. Some of our women have had the pleasure of seeing their sons and daughters follow in their careers, though they have not pressured to make that happen. Much more important for each of them is seeing their children carry on key Wisdom Trail principles of using their talents fully and sharing them with their community.

They recognize that the times they've lived through have had positive and negative impacts. Being a woman in a male-dominated environment toughened them, but they had to be careful not to reenforce the stereotype of the emasculating woman. Here was another place for balance, for displaying their feminine strengths of conciliation and empathy while learning to keep from being walked on.

Growing up during the Depression, our women knew what it meant to work hard and manage in hard times. Those lessons continued through the war years and engendered a lifelong appreciation of the distance they've come from scarcity and uncertainty, and of the opportunities that surfaced in peacetime and prosperity. Immigration has been another significant historical element in the twentieth century, and those who were immigrants or the children of immigrants were deeply influenced by that aspect of their lives. It fostered an intense drive for education as the surest avenue to success.

Despite the differences in where each woman's trail began, the common denominator among them is education. Almost all the women on the Wisdom Trail graduated from college. Those who did not, because they lacked the opportunity, have continued learning all their lives. They are models of the "returning woman," not to say the education junkie, who keeps going back to school when circumstances are right or when she discovers a promising new direction for her energy. Even if their college studies didn't lead directly to their vocation, they believe it would not have been possible without the foundation and impetus of education. This lesson is not lost on young women today, who are going on to higher education in numbers that have changed college gender ratios and expanded the fields in which women are taking their place.

Is the Wisdom Trail only for those who were born when the path was made thorny by the limits placed on women, and on their relations with men—limits that have now fallen away? Or are the qualities and values our women exhibit still timely? The sexual revolution has definitely altered the ways men and women connect today. Women are accepted in the workplace and in the professions; they have reached the top in the corporate world and aspire to the nation's highest political office. Yet many challenges and dilemmas still exist, perhaps in a different guise, and they still call for the values and qualities of the Wisdom Trail.

Our women demonstrate that it is possible to be an ordinary person, someone who accepts most of the basic values of our society, and yet to be a nonconformist, shaping the norms to meet individual goals and desires. The need for that capability has not lessened, only changed its form. It is still difficult for a woman to have a family and a career, still difficult for both men and women to accept what this entails to make a partnership work well. There are people still living out the stereotype of the emasculating woman and the autocratic man. The working world has not yet discovered a satisfactory way to facilitate equal partnerships, for example, through job sharing, parental leave for new fathers and mothers, and expanded opportunities for people to drop out and return to the work world. Good day care and after-school care are still scarce and costly.

The active countermovement of women opting out of careers and staying home to raise their children reflects the dilemma. These women are likely to return to the work world eventually, and it isn't clear that they will be welcomed. This is one area where the old norms worked in favor of the Wisdom Trail women, though they didn't know it at the time. Because they married under the old paradigm—marry young and have children right away—they were able to be at home while their children were small. When the children started school, the mothers were still young enough to start out on the next phase of their lives. They faced guilt and the pressure of time and social disapproval. But it seemed to work better than the more common pattern today, when women start a career first and then decide to have babies. The caveat of the old way is that it was important to have a bachelor's degree before marriage, and the downside was that young mothers with ambition to be out in the world were frustrated and bored at home with children. They couldn't know about the rich outside lives they would be making for themselves in a few years, or that they could succeed in having satisfying careers even later on.

But it still takes persistence to build a strong familial partnership, whether within marriage or outside of it, whether with the same or the opposite sex, whether romantic or companionable—the kind of persistence our women showed in teaching their families to accept their right to have goals of their own. It takes persistence to find the right avenue for a meaningful life's work when young people are expected to make this decision very early, persistence to keep a sense of possibility while acceding to today's demand to make a choice before they are ready to do so.

Adaptability is still necessary too, to recognize and respond to the needs of partners, and to fit one's talent and skills to the opportunities available, or to the lack of them. If opportunities weren't exactly knocking, our women employed their skill at improvising. They found ways to get their foot into hard-to-open doors or they went back to college for another degree to make them more employable. They are examples of the entrepreneurial spirit so crucial today, as jobs and whole industries change, appear, and disappear.

The quality of courage is needed at every age. It is still required for those who push into uncharted territory. In this day, when issues of ethics and fairness abound and the public is so much more aware of them, courage to stand up to power in the face of unfair or unethical behavior is called for. It takes courage too for working mothers to ask fathers and children to share more responsibility at home.

The spirit of service that was a beacon on the Wisdom Trail is having a renaissance in the twenty-first century. It's coming through new channels, for example, in the concept of "service learning" that is now a common requirement in high schools and a way to earn college credit. Young boys and girls are discovering firsthand the problems in our society, and they are experiencing and reporting on the "high" feeling that comes from participating in helping solve societal problems. Older people are opting to go into the Peace Corps; still-healthy retirees volunteer in social agencies. Those women and men who are juggling jobs and families may find it difficult to find time to give to others, but creative ways of introducing service into the workplace can be improvised. If the job does not offer a clear link to solving a community problem, people at work can be marshaled to support a charity by joining a weekend work party for Habitat for Humanity or by walking for a cure.

If women of today are to have it all, and if their partners are to share in the benefits of that goal, it is necessary to nourish the sense of connection, of loving and caring. It is the source of the deep relationships that continue to enrich the lives of the women whose stories are told here. These connections sustain these women in the remaining decades of their lives as through all the years before. They have done the heavy lifting necessary to hold any life partnership together, and to keep a web of friendships vital. From the death of a child to the death of a marriage, they held onto their capacity to love and go forward, focusing on the living and forgiving those who hurt them.

These women will tell you that without question their relationships are their most gratifying achievements. The knowledge that they have made a significant contribution to their world comes a close second.

THE PATHS OUR women took are silhouetted against their times, but today the trails—and the trials—are different. Trailblazers in the twenty-first century are making new paths, but they will find they call on the same qualities as those who went before them. In some ways things are easier, but in others they are harder. Working against widely held expectations gave our women a certain leverage that is not available today. Now marriage is much more egalitarian. Women are expected to share responsibility for the family income. The stakes for women who are workers and mothers are higher in both arenas. They are not only expected to fulfill the roles and responsibilities of parenthood, but are haunted by the myth of the superwoman. These "Soccer moms" are not only expected to cheer for their children, but to work and look sexy for their husbands. They are expected to do it all, and to do it well.

The positive side of these expectations is an expansion of opportunities. Women can be frank about how they want to live and what they want to do with their lives. Few fields are off limits. Although this expansion brings with it greater demands on their time, the Wisdom Trail skills of innovation, adaptation, courage are even more useful today. A woman must be innovative to fit all the pieces of her life into her schedule; she must adapt to make her time fit with those she wants to share it with; and she must be courageous in asking for equal consideration from those she loves.

As for making a contribution to society, the world is wide open. Expanded access increases the opportunities for service and the satisfaction that comes with it. Worldwide communication brings increased knowledge, and advances in travel have changed the venue for service from the neighborhood to the world. At the same time, local problems cry out for neighborhood solutions. Anyone looking for a cause need look no farther than the nearest community food bank, homeless shelter, teenage drop-out haven, or cancer lifeline programs. Public education is more demanding and more in need of dedicated professionals and volunteers than ever before. Politics have opened up for women, and cities, states, and the nation need women's qualities and skills.

The predicament for today's trailblazers is timing. When do you do what? Though it goes against the grain today, the life pattern of the Wisdom Trail women is worth considering: marrying early (preferably after earning a college degree) and having children first, then taking on the demands of the work world. Many women who opt for starting their career first and having children later are being entrepreneurial about finding part-time work while their children are small. Whatever the timetable, long-term satisfaction is served by choosing a career that provides a platform for service to the community. Health care and research, social work, education, diplomacy, politics, the arts—the opportunities to do well by doing good are infinite. There is still the volunteer route.

It may not give the same level of recognition, but it gives the same personal satisfaction.

Yet not every woman wants or will be able to find a career in a service profession, nor does everyone have the luxury of opting to move in and out of full-time work. Time for volunteering may not be in the cards for women who work long hours and have heavy home responsibilities. Lengthened life spans and changing economic times are necessitating longer years of work, especially for those who must support themselves and their families. For those fortunate enough to retain their health when they retire, the opportunity for service to the community will be waiting. Then the personal dividends accrued by helping to solve social problems will be compounded by the new relationships that develop in this type of work.

Wisdom Trail women grew up when the prescribed role for women could lead to acquiescence or to opportunity. These women chose opportunity. They seized what openings they found and carved out areas of accomplishment. As society came to accept broader roles for them, they came to be seen as the women's movement at its best: a force for solidarity with humankind.

The present is soon history. The way of the Wisdom Trail is already history. But the women who blazed it are still forging into the future with the strengths that have carried them so far. Their light shines backward—because what matters is the qualities you bring to the journey, and forward—because trailblazing is open to everyone. Pick your area, gather your credentials, stuff your backpack, and go out into the friendly wilderness, where the footsteps of others are visible and there is still plenty of opportunity to blaze a new trail.

Acknowledgments

Janet Lieberman

My deepest appreciation goes to the women who were willing to share their life experiences with me and made this book a reality. Their trust, bravery, faith, wit, and intelligence made the stories in this book possible and real. I am grateful to Lorraine Beitler, Ruth Feder, Selma Fink, Emily Korzenik, Shirley Medalie, and Joyce Millington for allowing me to interview them.

I also want to express my sincerest gratitude to my secretary, Solange Pereira, whose support and expertise made this book possible. Her interest and enthusiasm, as well as her skills and tireless devotion, were essential to our effort.

My sincerest thanks to the professionals who made this idea into a book. Melanie Jackson, our agent, smoothed the process using her expertise to guide us and help us succeed. Ann Godoff, the publisher of the Penguin Press, provided the inspiration and created the support to make this book a reality.

Finally, thanks to all my friends and supporters who collaborated and encouraged my effort and particularly to Bernard Schechtman, my accountant and adviser, who is enthusiastic about the book and encourages me with his interest and positive expectations.

Julie Hungar

I am deeply grateful to the women who agreed to be a part of *The Wisdom Trail*. They have shared their memories with unbelievable generosity and candor. Hearing their stories has been awe-inspiring; only less so has been the challenge of trying to bring that inspiration onto the page. I have certainly not done them full justice. These are the remarkable women I interviewed, and I thank them for giving me the privilege of listening in on their lives: Nell Berry, Jeanne Bluechel, Sister Madonna Buder, June Chen, Alice Dieter, Elaine Hayes, Ruth Lubic, Jean Phillips, Mary Jane Stevenson, Claudia Thomas, Charlotte Ward, Debby Wing, Alice Yee, "Patricia Radcliffe," (whose openness I have honored by giving her another name), and, of course, Janet Lieberman.

None of the interviews would have been possible without the people who told me about and helped me contact these women. For making the essential connections, I am grateful to Ron Stoneham, Debbie Ehrlichman, Ellomae DeMond, Mimi Yong, Phyllis Edmundson, Harriet Cody, Jaye Letson Hungar, Joan Ray, Linda Willenberg, Paula Hungar, and Alice Yee. Alice put me in contact with her colleagues from Peaceful Valley, who kindly allowed me to meet with and interview them by telephone, and she helped me immeasurably with their stories as well. When I visited Charlotte Ward in Alabama, she brought together a group of her friends, all of whom have interesting lives and share the distinction of being members of Phi Beta Kappa. Unfortunately for the book, my minimal technical skills were defeated by the challenge of capturing them on tape all at once, and I was not able to use anything from that delightful afternoon. My apologies to the women of Auburn Phi Beta Kappa—they had wonderful stories too.

We have been fortunate in having Melanie Jackson as our agent; she has steered us through the publishing process with understanding, expertise, and patience. The support of Ann Godoff, the publisher of the Penguin Press, has been essential and immensely reassuring. I am especially grateful to our wonderful, brilliant editor, Vanessa Mobley—wonderful because she was so gently helpful and optimistic in pulling us along during the writing, and brilliant because she waited until she knew we would actually finish and then gave us expert direction for the hard work of fixing what didn't work. Along the way, she provided structure for the book and great ideas for ways to make it better. Her assistant, Nicole Hughes, has given sterling support, helping to make our pathway clear and smooth. The book is much more readable than it would have been without the copyediting of Rachel Burd and Jane Carolina.

I am grateful for family members and friends who put up with me and cheered me on through this whole long process. My grown-up children—Ann, Susan, Tom, and Paula and their spouses—have given me understanding, love, and support to help me keep going. Finally, the real reason I agreed to do this tempting but demanding project was that my husband, Gordon, encouraged me to accept the challenge. Had he lived, he would have read every word of the manuscript, and he would have thought it was great.

Dr. Janet Lieberman is a psychologist and award-winning educator. Among the numerous awards she has received for her dedication to creating opportunities for the underserved are the Charles A. Dana Award in Higher Education and the McGraw-Hill Prize in Education. She currently consults at LaGuardia Community College.

Dr. Julie Hungar is vice chancellor emeritus of the Seattle Community colleges. She is a consultant in strategic planning for higher education, and is currently engaged in a study of single-sex education in middle schools.